BLOOM'S ReViews

COMPREHENSIVE **RESEARCH & STUDY GUIDES**

F. Scott Fitzgerald's

The Great Gatsby

Edited & with
an Introduction
by Harold Bloom

First Printing
1 3 5 7 9 8 6 4 2

The Chelsea House World Wide Web site address is
http://www.chelseahouse.com

ISBN 0-7910-3676-6 (hc)   ISBN 0-7910-4124-7 (pb)

Chelsea House Publishers
1974 Sproul Road, Suite 400
P.O. Box 914
Broomall, PA 19008-0914

Contents

Editor's Note

My Introduction centers upon what makes Gatsby great and finds that eminence in his Platonic ability to transcend the ironies of his own life. Critical Views begin with an exchange between Scott Fitzgerald and his editor, Maxwell E. Perkins, in which the author defends his Platonized "vagueness" in portraying Jay Gatsby.

Various senses of Gatsby as a symbol of American "failure" are argued by Alfred Kazin, Maxwell Geismar, and Edwin Fussell. A. E. Dyson asserts instead that Gatsby fails only in a relative way, one that makes him a tragic hero, a view maintained also by Brian Way, and by Joan M. Allen's finding of Christological elements in Fitzgerald's protagonist.

The emphasis turns to Daisy with Judith Fetterly, who sees that vacuous beauty as Gatsby's self-validation. Nick Carraway's vernacular eloquence is emphasized by George Garrett, after which Daisy returns in Sarah Fryer's defense of the heroine's vulnerability.

Romance elements in *The Great Gatsby* are discussed by Jerome Mandel, who sees the hero as a type of the courtly lover. Jay Gatsby's kinship to the narrator Nick Carraway is judged by Joyce Rowe as a shared self-division, while Richard Lehan compares Fitzgerald's cosmic pessimism to similar stances in T. S. Eliot and Oswald Spengler.

In the concluding extract, Andrew Hook compares Tom Buchanan, a brutal embodiment of a Yale University now fortunately extinct, to Gatsby, discovering in each a midwestern pseudo-aristocracy hardly preferable to the authentic eastern social class.

Introduction

HAROLD BLOOM

The Great Gatsby has only a few rivals as the great American novel of the twentieth century; doubtless they would include works by Faulkner, Hemingway, Cather, and Dreiser. Formal shaping is one of the many aesthetic virtues of F. Scott Fitzgerald's masterwork: style, characterization, and plot are all superbly balanced to achieve a highly unified end. Rereading the book, yet once more, my initial and prime reaction is pleasure renewed; it is as though *The Great Gatsby*'s freshness never can wear off. Though it is regarded as the classic of what Fitzgerald himself permanently named the Jazz Age, the novel is anything but a "period piece." As our century nears conclusion, the relevance of *The Great Gatsby* increases, because it is the definitive romance of the American dream, a concept or vision that haunts our society. Critics differ as to whether the theme of the novel is "the withering of the American dream," as Marius Bewley argued, or else a celebration of a Romantic hope in America despite all the ugly realities. Fitzgerald himself, as much a High Romantic as his favorite poet, John Keats, was too great an artist not to entertain both possibilities. In one register, *The Great Gatsby* is a companion work to T. S. Eliot's *The Waste Land,* a desolate vision of a world without faith or order. And yet, in a finer tone, the novel keeps faith with Jay Gatsby's dream of a perfect love, of a fulfillment that transcends the absurdity of Daisy, who in herself is hardly a fit representative of Gatsby's idealized yearnings.

Bewley shrewdly sees Fitzgerald's involvement in Gatsby's aspirations, but again Bewley argues that Gatsby's death is also a spiritual failure. A reader can be legitimately uncertain as to exactly how Gatsby ought to be apprehended. Much depends upon how much the reader places himself under the control of the novel's narrator, Nick Carraway. By mediating Gatsby for us, precisely in the way that Joseph Conrad's Marlow mediates Jim in *Lord Jim* or Kurtz in *Heart of Darkness,* Carraway's consciousness dominates the novel, and Carraway is no more Fitzgerald than Marlow is Conrad. Marlow's Romanticism is echoed by

Carraway's, though Marlow rarely gets in the way of the story's progress, while Carraway frequently does. It is not clear how Fitzgerald wished us to regard Carraway's sometimes less than subtle ironies, but I suspect that they are devices for distancing the novelist from his fictive narrator. Carraway is a very decent fellow, but he does not transcend the fashions of his time and place, as Fitzgerald does. This limitation is one of Carraway's ultimate strengths, because it allows him his own dream of Jay Gatsby as the Romantic hero of the American experience. Fitzgerald, like Conrad before him, regards the deep self as unknowable; Carraway in contrast finds in Gatsby "some heightened sensitivity to the promises of life." The English critic Malcolm Bradbury memorably termed Gatsby "a coarse Platonist," yet any Platonist ultimately is not a materialist. Since Gatsby's dream of love depends upon an alchemy that meta-morphoses wealth into eros, we can be reminded of Emerson's wonderful irony: "Money, in some of its effects, is as beautiful as roses."

Gatsby's greatest strength is a "Platonic conception of him-self," which gives him the hope that he can roll back time, that he and the unlikely Daisy can somehow be as Adam and Eve early in the morning. Despite the absurd distance of this dream from reality, Gatsby never yields up his hope. That refusal to surrender to reality kills him, yet it also gives him his peculiar greatness, justifying the book's title as being more than an irony. Gatsby's refusal of history is profoundly Emersonian, though doubtless Gatsby had never heard of Emerson. Edith Wharton told Fitzgerald, in a letter, that "to make Gatsby really great, you ought to have given us his early career." Perhaps, but that is to forget that we know only Carraway's Gatsby, the finished product of an American quest, and a figure curiously beyond judgment. Actually Fitzgerald had written what we now know as the short story "Absolution" to serve as a picture of Gatsby's early life, but he decided to omit it from the novel so as to preserve some sense of mystery about his hero. Mystery certainly remains: Gatsby's death, though squalid, transfigures him in the reader's imagination. The dreamer dies, so that an image, however grotesque, of the American dream can continue to live. It is not possible that Gatsby dies as a vi-carious atonement for the reader, and yet that may be Gatsby's function in regard to Carraway. Nick goes west at the book's conclusion still sustained by the idealism of Gatsby's effect upon him.

It is one of Fitzgerald's oddest triumphs that we accept his vision of Gatsby's permanent innocence; the gross reality of Daisy's love for her brutal husband, Tom Buchanan, is dismissed by Gatsby as merely "personal" and as something that can be canceled by a simple denial. We come to understand that Gatsby is in love neither with Daisy nor with love itself, but rather with a moment out of time that he persuades himself he shared with Daisy. Gangster and dreamer, Gatsby is more of an inarticulate American poet than he is an episode in the later history of American transcendentalism. Since Fitzgerald is so superbly articulate a writer, Carraway again is necessary as a mediator between the author and his tragic hero. Gatsby's vitalism, his wonderful capacity for hope, is enhanced when Fitzgerald compares him to the endlessly recalcitrant Carraway, whose non-relationship with Jordan Baker heightens our sense of the sexual ambiguity of both characters. What moves Carraway about Gatsby is the image of generosity, of having given oneself away to a dream. Fitzgerald makes us suspect that Gatsby, unlike Carraway, is not deceived altogether by his own dreaming. However inarticulate his own poetic vision is, Gatsby seems to grasp that Daisy indeed is *his* fiction. To believe in your own fiction, while knowing it to be a fiction, is the nicer knowledge of belief, according to Wallace Stevens, who was not being ironic. Gatsby also transcends the ironies of his own story, and so earns his greatness. ❖

Biography of F. Scott Fitzgerald

Francis Scott Key Fitzgerald was born into a well-to-do merchant famlly in St. Paul, Minnesota, on September 24, 1896. During the first twelve years of Fitzgerald's life his family lived in Buffalo and Syracuse, New York, before moving back to St. Paul. Fitzgerald took to writing early, publishing his first story in 1909 in *Now and Then,* the school magazine of St. Paul Academy. He then attended the Newman School in Hackensack, New Jersey, before moving on to Princeton University, where he remained sporadically from 1913 to 1917. Fitzgerald spent his college years in socializing (it was here that he became friends with fellow student Edmund Wilson, who later became a distinguished critic), writing librettos for school musicals, and producing the first draft of his novel *This Side of Paradise,* but he did poorly in his studies and left without a degree.

Fitzgerald joined the U.S. Army, where he remained for just over a year. He was stationed mostly at Camp Sheridan near Montgomery, Alabama, and it was here that he met Zelda Sayre, whom he would later marry. Discharged in early 1919, Fitzgerald moved to New York City to work in an advertising agency and write. His early literary ambitions found their first fulfillment at this time with the publication of stories in *Smart Set, Scribner's Magazine,* and other fashionable periodicals. *This Side of Paradise,* a story of college life that is not considered one of Fitzgerald's best works, was published in 1920 and was very well received. This rapid rise to fame allowed Fitzgerald to marry Zelda Sayre in 1920 and visit Europe with her the following year. Their only child, Frances Scott Fitzgerald, was born in 1921.

Back in America, the Fitzgeralds became leading lights in the hectic social life of New York, and were featured in society and gossip magazines. In spite of writing and selling numerous stories, brought together in the collections *Flappers and Philosophers* (1920), *Tales of the Jazz Age* (1922), and *All the Sad Young Men* (1926), the Fitzgeralds lived perpetually on the brink of financial disaster because of their extravagant lifestyle. *The Beautiful and Damned* (1922), a satire on the younger generation, was highly regarded, but the play *The Vegetable* (1923) received very poor reviews and never made it to Broadway.

Fitzgerald spent most of the period from 1924 to 1931 in Europe, where he completed *The Great Gatsby* (1925), a novel of high society in Long Island that is now regarded as his finest work and one of the great novels in American literature. But in spite of Fitzgerald's own belief that this work was his masterpiece, sales and reviews were disappointing. Back in America, he worked briefly as a screenwriter in Hollywood in 1927, and continued to live on his short stories. The latter part of Fitzgerald's residence in Europe (1929–31) was darkened by his increasing dependence on alcohol and his wife's mental instability. Zelda actually broke down in 1930, and after the Fitzgeralds' return to America she spent the next several years in sanitariums. Fitzgerald described this entire difficult period in such essays as "The Crack-Up," "Pasting It Together," and "Handle with Care."

Living mostly in Rodgers Forge, near Baltimore, Maryland, Fitzgerald managed to write a third novel, *Tender Is the Night,* for serialization in *Scribner's Magazine* in 1934; it was slightly revised for its book publication later that same year. This novel about a psychiatrist and his schizophrenic wife draws heavily upon Fitzgerald's own life and travels in Europe. A short story collection, *Taps at Reveille* (1935), followed. In 1935 Fitzgerald suffered a recurrence of the tuberculosis that had afflicted him in youth. Struggling with ill-health, alcoholism, and debts, Fitzgerald in 1937 found it necessary to return to Hollywood, where he signed a contract with MGM. His career was not especially distinguished, although he did work on *Gone with the Wind* and other important films; he also continued to write short stories.

On December 1, 1940, Fitzgerald suffered a heart attack, but he continued to work frenetically on his last novel, *The Last Tycoon,* the story of a motion picture mogul. Another heart attack occurred a few weeks later, and he died on December 21, 1940, leaving *The Last Tycoon* unfinished; it was published posthumously in 1941. Zelda Sayre Fitzgerald died in a fire at the Highland Sanitarium, near Asheville, North Carolina, on March 11, 1947. ❖

Thematic and Structural Analysis

The Great Gatsby begins as a confession. It is a tale told in retrospect by Nick Carraway who looks back to the previous year when he lived in New York City. At the outset, he recalls the advice his father gave him as a child to refrain from criticizing people who have not had the advantages of a privileged upbringing. He suggests that as he grew older this habit of reserving judgment availed him of the unofficial role of confessor, to whom "wild, unknown men" would open their hearts. But he admits that the events of last year have hardened him against listening to the "aborted sorrows" and "short-winded elations" of these men, with the single exception of Jay Gatsby. Since Gatsby was the central figure around whom the events in Nick's life in New York occurred, he feels compelled to tell the reader the story of Gatsby's demise. The story of Gatsby's life is the exception for Nick because he closely identifies with the romantic plight of the title character. The logic of the narrative frame in which Nick confides to us as Gatsby confided in him thus implies that we should read the tale which follows as parallel to events in Nick's own psychological development.

The action of the story begins when Nick comes east from a midwestern city to join a brokerage firm and earn a living. He moves into a "weatherbeaten cardboard bungalow" just off the Long Island Sound in West Egg. His ramshackle cottage is sandwiched between much larger mansions of the nouveau riche. Next door is "a colossal affair" built in imitation of a French hotel, complete with a marble swimming pool and forty acres of gardens and lawn which sweep down toward the water. The house belongs to Gatsby; although when Nick moves there he only knows the name, not the man.

Across a small bay lies the village of East Egg whose coastline is speckled with the "white palaces" of the more blue-blooded wealthy. Nick's second cousin once removed, Daisy, lives there with her husband, Tom Buchanan. On an early summer evening Nick drives over to the Buchanan house to have dinner. The warm, golden light of the afternoon reflects off the

French windows of the Buchanan's Georgian Colonial mansion and resonates within Nick a sense of well-being. And yet he feels as though he has entered a fairy tale gone horribly awry. Tom greets him out front with the foreboding air of a predator welcoming his next prey, and when Nick enters the house he claims to find Daisy and her friend, Jordan Baker, seemingly aloft in the sea breeze which blows in off the sound and buoys up their white dresses. Eerily, everything in the room looks as though it were about to fly up to "the frosted wedding cake of a ceiling" until Tom slams the windows shut. With the air now caught in the room, the furniture and the two women seem to slowly balloon to the floor.

The order of these two events—Nick investing the aura around Daisy with a fantastic quality, and Tom's ability to deflate that romantic moment—presents a microcosm of the narrative as a whole. The rest of the evening at the Buchanan's conforms to this pattern. It is a travesty of domestic harmony. Daisy does her best to conceal the all too obvious signs of marital strife by flitting from one topic of conversation to another. She asks Nick about people back home in the Midwest, and she gushes forth patter about her childhood and how Nick looks like a perfect rose. But these insincere attempts at levity only serve to emphasize the strain between her and Tom. In a particularly barbed exchange Fitzgerald represents the struggle for emotional control of their marriage as a kind of oppression. Tom tells Nick that he has been reading racist literature which, he claims, scientifically proves that white supremacy is best for the world order. Daisy tries to turn Tom's words against him with the suggestion that his stupidity and brutish insensitivity make him like a baboon, "a great, big, hulking physical specimen."

The evening finally reaches a moment of crisis when Tom leaves the table to speak to his mistress on the telephone. Daisy follows him into the house from the veranda where Nick and Jordan listen intently for sounds of a fight. Tom and Daisy return as though nothing has happened, but the dinner soon dissolves with Daisy walking off into the "velvet dusk." Nick begins to sense that the rules of life for the fabulously rich are uncomfortably different from his own. Squelching his somewhat comic instinct to call for the police, he returns home to spy his notorious and yet mysterious neighbor, Gatsby, standing alone in his yard looking across the water at a faint, green dock light. At dinner, Jordan had asked if Nick lived near this man, who has a reputation for throwing one lavish party after another. Nick remembers that Daisy appeared to recognize Gatsby's name but made little mention of it. Looking out across the water himself, Nick wonders at the significance of the green light and then, turning back to the shore, realizes that Gatsby has disappeared.

The opening of **Chapter II** foregrounds the symbolic importance of geography in the novel. The villages of West Egg and East Egg are separated by "the valley of ashes," an industrialized wasteland. Presiding over this valley are the vast, unblinking eyes of Dr. T. J. Eckleburg, whose one-yard-high retinas stare down from behind "enormous yellow spectacles" at the dim landscape of tract housing, mindlessly toiling men, and rising smog. The eyes are a remnant from some oculist's billboard-size advertisement of his wares, but they also embody an attitude of eyes-wide-open realism and modern disenchantment. By comparison, West Egg is the locale of the American dream in miniature and East Egg is the home of those who are longtime captains of industry. Nick trades upon the vocabulary of the American frontier in the first chapter when his ability to direct someone to West Egg village makes him feel like "a guide, a pathfinder, an original settler." And the fact that Gatsby owns a homesteader's allotment of forty acres informs this small part of Long Island with the vast, mythical promise of the American West.

The rest of **Chapter II** details Tom's life with his mistress. On their way to Manhattan, Tom drags Nick off the train into the valley of ashes to meet "his girl," Myrtle Wilson. Myrtle and her husband George live above a decrepit garage and car-repair shop. Tom stops briefly to tease George Wilson about his business and then arranges to meet his wife in New York. The scenes which follow record the sordid and brutal nature of their affair. Tom has an apartment on the Upper West Side where he and Myrtle entertain a small group of friends. Tom appears to derive perverse glee as he watches Myrtle and the people she invites act as though they are living the high life. They drink heavily and make ignorant small talk about fashion and art. The evening ends when Myrtle utters Daisy's name one too many times and Tom breaks her nose with the flat of his hand. Nick stumbles from the apartment and catches a train back to Long Island.

Chapter III consists of two distinct sections. The first and longer section occurs at one of Gatsby's famous parties and presents a distinct lyrical comparison with Tom and Myrtle's bitter soiree. Gatsby employs a corps of caterers and eight servants to feed the continual flow of guests, invited and uninvited, who appear every summer evening as the sun begins to go down. A hired orchestra plays the latest jazz tunes and long banquet tables are spread with country hams, succulent turkeys, leafy mountains of salad, and a cornucopia of hors d'oeuvres. A fully stocked bar, complete with brass rail, stands in the main hall of the house and offers a profusion of long-forgotten cocktails. The guests loosen up with each passing round of drinks and begin to mingle, dance, and whirl themselves into a prolonged state of manic joy.

When Nick arrives he is daunted somewhat by the sheer number of anonymous merrymakers who have come to what Gatsby's chauffeur had called a "little party." He slinks off toward a table of cocktails to disguise the fact that he is alone, and is well on his way to getting "roaring drunk" when he spies the familiar face of Jordan Baker. He approaches her and expresses his concern that he has been unable to find the host in order to thank him for the invitation. Jordan takes him by the hand for the rest of the evening and helps him navigate the banal and self-indulgent conversations of the other partygoers as they look for the host.

Gatsby's absence is virtually the theme of the party. Wild rumors about his background and the mysterious source of his enormous wealth circulate like currency among the guests. One person heard that he killed a man, another that he was a German spy during the Great War. Whatever Gatsby is or was, it is clear that he will go to extraordinary lengths to avoid trouble, spending extravagant amounts of money to ensure good will. His house is impeccably decorated to suggest he is a man of great accomplishment. But, as one owl-eyed, drunken man notes when Nick and Jordan enter the library, the pages of the books are uncut.

Nick resigns himself to drinking fishbowls of champagne and watching the increasing raucousness of the party without meeting Gatsby. He sits with Jordan and another man his age at a table as an Italian tenor sings to the crowd. The other man at the table claims to recognize Nick from the war and asks him to ride his new hydroplane in the morning. Nick confesses to him how awkward he feels being at a party where he has yet to meet the host. The man guffaws and then says, "I'm Gatsby." He calmly smiles at Nick and reassures him that it is a common mistake. He conveys a warm sense of spiritual kinship, and yet Nick feels as though he chooses his words with too much care.

Gatsby is called to the phone on business and soon after sends his butler to ask Jordan to meet with him alone. Nick wanders around the flagging party which has begun to break up into jealous squabbles among husbands, wives, mistresses, and paramours. He sees Gatsby and Jordan emerge from the library as though they had been engaged in something suspicious and then takes his leave. Outside a departing guest has crashed his car into a ditch but is too drunk to understand what has happened. He tries to enlist everyone's help to push it back on the road even though one of the wheels has sheered off. The absurdity of this scene, in which Fitzgerald ties the recklessness of the rich to the mishandling of automobiles, foreshadows events to come.

The shorter section of **Chapter III** repeats the same theme of recklessness, but this time in the context of a romance. Nick reports his growing excitement for life in the city and begins to develop an attraction, a "tender curiosity," for Jordan. But he soon discovers that she is less than trustworthy. She leaves the top of a borrowed car down in the rain and lies about it. This act reminds Nick that Jordan had been accused of cheating during a golf tournament a few years back. He senses once again that his careful, middle-class nature is at odds with the recklessness of the rich. This fact is brought home when Jordan passes so close to a pedestrian in her car that she flicks a button off the man's coat. When Nick questions her about her carelessness, she agrees that she is careless but then replies that "it takes two to make an accident."

Chapter IV opens with a famous jazzlike litany of the names of the guests who frequent Gatsby's parties. Nick comments that one cannot find any pattern to the names, or anything which would help bring the character of Gatsby into focus. The rest of the chapter, however, would appear to provide just the sort of background material needed to know who Jay Gatsby really is.

Gatsby invites Nick to lunch with him in Manhattan. As they ride up together in his sumptuous, cream-colored car Gatsby tells his life story to Nick. He says that the rumors about his being a bootlegger or a murderer are false, and that he wants to square his reputation so that Nick will be willing to do him a favor. He claims to be the sole inheritor of his family's fortune and that he has been educated, according to tradition, at Oxford. He builds a grandiose picture of himself in the years after college. He maintains that he lived like a "young rajah" in the capitals of Europe—collecting rubies, hunting big game, and painting. The outbreak of the Great War brought him relief from his life as a dilettante and he says that he "tried very hard to die." But fate seemed to be against him. He claims that he fought so valiantly in the Argonne Forest that every Allied government awarded him a decoration. In order to prove his story Gatsby shows a photograph of himself in front of an archway at Oxford and one of the many medals he supposedly earned during the course of the war.

Gatsby's tale almost beguiles Nick, but the scene which immediately follows their drive to the city raises doubts about the truthfulness of Gatsby's story. At lunch he introduces Nick to Meyer Wolfsheim, a "friend," who mistakes Nick for someone looking to enter the world of organized crime. Wolfsheim wears cufflinks made from human molars and regales Nick with stories about gangland slayings and payoffs. When Wolfsheim leaves, Nick sarcastically asks if he is a dentist and is flabbergasted when Gatsby claims that Wolfsheim is "the man who fixed the World Series back in 1919." As Nick and Gatsby get up to leave, Nick spots Tom Buchanan across the restaurant.

But when he stops off to introduce Gatsby he turns to find that his enigmatic friend has disappeared.

The reason for Gatsby's odd exit and the key to the entire plot become evident in the final scene of Chapter IV. Over afternoon tea, Jordan Baker tells Nick that Gatsby and Daisy had been in love before Daisy married Tom Buchanan. They had met before the war when Gatsby was a young lieutenant stationed in Louisville. But when he went off to fight in Europe, Daisy's social life as a southern belle carried on. Shortly after her debut she married the fabulously wealthy Tom, despite the fact that she still loved Gatsby. Jordan tells Nick that on the eve of the wedding, Daisy was found in her bedroom "drunk as a monkey," with a letter in her hands. She wanted to call the wedding off, but failed. Daisy's life moved on and she lost track of Gatsby until that evening when Jordan asked if Nick lived near him.

Jordan's story clarifies the mysterious character of Gatsby for Nick. He realizes that the apparent "purposeless splendor" of his neighbor's life is really all part of a glorious romantic quest for the dreamlike love of his youth. He learns that Gatsby bought the house directly across the bay from Daisy's home just to be near her, and that Gatsby throws his lavish parties with the sole hope of attracting her attention. Although Nick initially resists the idea of helping Gatsby court Daisy anew, he identifies with the boundless sense of possibility which Gatsby's life exemplifies. The chapter ends with Nick paradoxically taking solace in the practicality of his relationship with Jordan even as he agrees to invite Daisy over to his house to meet Gatsby.

Chapter V mainly records the reunion of Gatsby and Daisy. When it begins a seemingly forlorn Gatsby makes a couple of feeble attempts to bond with Nick, and fumblingly thanks him for his help in bringing Daisy nearer. Nick bridles somewhat at the crassness which shows through the veneer of his neighbor's visionary desire. Gatsby overdoes the preparations for the tea. He sends a "greenhouse" of flowers to decorate Nick's humble cottage but then almost flees the scene when Daisy arrives. The first moments of their reunion are quite tense and Nick worries that it is going to be a disaster. He escapes the room and leaves them alone for a while. When he returns he finds Daisy teary-eyed and Gatsby aglow with exultation. The three of them cross Nick's yard to take a tour of Gatsby's house.

With the culmination of his romantic quest at hand, Gatsby exudes confidence as he guides Daisy and Nick through a fetishistic inventory of his possessions. It climaxes in one of the most ironically pathetic scenes in American literature when Gatsby displays pile after pile of silk, flannel, and linen shirts to his guests. Daisy sobs, "They're such beautiful shirts. . . . It makes me sad because I have never seen such—such beautiful shirts before." At moments Nick seems to catch a glimpse of disappointment on Gatsby's face as though the reality of Daisy did not measure up to the dream of her, but these expressions fade as they speak softly to one another. Nick departs, leaving them together to listen to a pianist's hasty renditions of popular love ballads.

The rise of Jay Gatsby through the first five chapters begins to unravel in **Chapter VI**. Nick exposes the truth about his neighbor. His real name is James Gatz, and he is the son of "shiftless and unsuccessful farm people." Never educated, but wildly ambitious and sensitive to the romantic possibilities inherent in the American dream, he crafted an image of himself as a man who belonged to the upper reaches of society. Fortune smiled on Gatz in the form of Dan Cody, a rough-and-tumble mining magnate, who had gone from rags to riches. Gatsby saw a drunken Cody anchor his yacht in the shallows of Lake Superior. Seizing the opportunity to warn Cody off the rocks, he rowed out to the boat and charmed his way on deck. Once aboard Gatz became Gatsby and he toured the seas with Cody for five years until Cody died. Nick reveals that Gatsby inherited no money from Cody, but rather he secured a much more valuable legacy—the indomitable spirit of a millionaire.

This information intrudes into the flow of events, for Nick admits that he only learned the truth about his neighbor much later. But the intrusion of the reality about Gatsby heightens the sense of the grandness of his gestures. Just as quickly as Nick undercuts his friend's character, he buoys him back up in order to detail the growing contest between Tom and Gatsby for

Daisy's affections. When Tom learns that Daisy has been seeing more of Gatsby than would seem proper, he accompanies her to one of his rival's parties. The remainder of **Chapter VI** engages in an extended metaphor that compares Gatsby's impulse to construct a self-image with the making of movies. A menagerie of famous people from the movie-making business grace the evening with the air of the unreal, as if the host and his guests had walked right out of a film. But the fantasy in which Daisy might be like the "gorgeous, scarcely human orchid" of a starlet, and in which Gatsby might fulfill his larger-than-life expectations, dissolves before the reality of the sordid and lewd behavior of the partygoers. Everyone is too drunk and too loud, and the evening ends on a bitter note. Tom chases after another woman. Daisy is miserable. The scene differs remarkably from the clip of lyric memory which closes the chapter, when Gatsby first kissed Daisy five years ago and "at his lips' touch she blossomed for him like a flower."

Things literally heat up in **Chapter VII**. Such a grimy, summer swelter descends upon New York that Nick says he cannot imagine anyone caring about romance. But on an unbearable hot afternoon Tom and Daisy invite Nick, Gatsby, and Jordan Baker over to their house for cocktails and dinner. Afterwards, they drive into Manhattan. Tom, who is driving Gatsby's yellow car, stops off at the Wilsons to buy some gas and discovers that Mr. Wilson is ill. He has learned that Myrtle is having an affair and has decided to move out West to tear her away from her lover. Nick notices Myrtle peering out from an upstairs window and surmises that she thinks Jordan is Tom's wife. Tom grows angry and speeds away to catch Gatsby and Daisy, who are riding together in Tom's blue coupé. When they rendezvous everyone agrees to go to the Plaza for drinks, and maybe to take cool baths. Nick notices that Tom is panicked by the fact that he appears to be losing both of the women in his life.

Once all five of them are alone in a hotel room, they hear the sounds of a wedding occurring in the ballroom below, and conversation turns to the day of Daisy's own wedding. Tom becomes priggish and hypocritical and begins to argue with Gatsby. He complains that Gatsby is trying to break up his happy home and that he won't stand for it. Gatsby insists that

Daisy tell Tom that she has never loved him, that she has only ever loved Gatsby, and that she wants a divorce. Daisy hesitantly complies until Tom exposes Gatsby for the uneducated, bootlegger that he is. She then admits that she loves both men, a fact which satisfies Tom but disappoints Gatsby. With tempers aflare, the party breaks up with Gatsby and Daisy driving back to Long Island in his car, and the rest in Tom's car.

When Tom, Nick, and Jordan pass back by the Wilson's garage they see that there has been an accident. Witnesses say that Myrtle Wilson came running out of the garage onto the road, yelling and waving at a passing, yellow car. The car hit her without stopping. Mr. Wilson thinks that it was the car which he saw Tom driving earlier that killed his wife, but Tom proves that he has just arrived in his blue coupé. When Tom, Nick, and Jordan leave, Tom starts to cry and whimpers about how Gatsby is a coward to have left the scene of the accident.

They arrive back at the Buchanan's to see Daisy's light on. Tom and Jordan enter the house, but Nick, disgusted by the whole affair, waits outside for a taxi. He finds Gatsby lurking in the bushes nearby. Gatsby asks about the accident and unwittingly divulges that Daisy had actually been the driver of the "death car," as the newspapers called it the next day. He tells Nick that he is waiting to make sure that Tom does not try to brutalize Daisy because of "that unpleasantness this afternoon." To reassure Gatsby that nothing will happen to Daisy, Nick tiptoes up to the kitchen window and sees Tom and Daisy engaged in a calm, intense, intimate conversation. They are holding hands and Nick realizes that although they are not happy, they are not unhappy. They look as though they are conspiring together, and Nick thinks that Daisy may have told Tom the truth about the accident. He walks back to tell Gatsby that everything is quiet inside, but Gatsby refuses to leave. He persists to stand alone, a forlorn lover in the moonlight, "watching over nothing."

The next day Nick finds Gatsby at home and suggests that he go away until things cool off. But his neighbor still clutches at the hope that Daisy will leave Tom. Shaken by the exposure of his lies and yesterday's accident, Gatsby confesses everything about his youth to Nick. In the first part of **Chapter VIII** he recounts those few happy days five years ago in Louisville. He had traded falsely on the glorious illusions of what his future would be after the war in order to win her body more than her heart, but found that he had fallen in love despite himself. Daisy became tantamount to "a grail" for him, even as she "vanished into her rich house, into her rich, full life, leaving Gatsby—nothing." He truly had been a war hero, but by the time he arrived back in the United States Daisy had married Tom. Since then Gatsby had trailed after her in the hope that he could renew the romantic promise of the past.

Nick leaves Gatsby, who is about to take a swim, to go to the city for work. He really sympathizes with the hopeless plight of a dreamer like Gatsby, and he finds it hard to think of anything else. Disgusted with the invulnerable recklessness of the rich, he breaks off his relationship with Jordan and tries to return hastily to his neighbor's side. But while he is at work George Wilson also makes his way to Gatsby's manor. Deranged by the loss of his wife, Wilson pursues the owner of the mysterious yellow car. Sure that this owner must also be the man who broke Myrtle's nose he goes to exact revenge. He finds Gatsby afloat on a pneumatic mattress in the swimming pool, and he shoots him. Then he turns the gun upon himself.

The **last chapter** in the story of the Great Gatsby records his return to obscurity. Nick tries desperately to find people who will attend the funeral, but he fails to raise a single soul. Wolfsheim wants to avoid any connection and advises Nick that it is better "to show our friendship for a man when he is alive and not after he is dead." Tom and Daisy leave for a vacation without warning and leave no forwarding address. Only Henry C. Gatz, Gatsby's father, arrives to help bury his son. The older Gatz proudly admires his son's rise into prominence in the East, and mistakenly sees him as one of the great builders of America. Nick realizes the frailty of the father's perception when it is clear that a wrinkled photograph which his son sent him of his mansion has more reality to him than the mansion itself. Mr. Gatz then shows Nick a schedule for self-improvement, which he found in the back of a book called *Hopalong Cassidy,* that James Gatz had made as a young boy. Replete with an admonition against smoking and a plan to practice elocution and poise for an hour a day, the schedule reveals the sad, meager, but earnest resolutions of a boy on the very fringe of the American dream.

Nick concludes his narrative with a series of confessions that make clear his own identification with Jay Gatsby. He realizes that his story had really been a story about the American West, about the land of opportunity. He remembers the lyric moments of his childhood when, arriving home for Christmas holidays, he and his peers felt "unutterably aware of our identity with this country." He understands now that Gatsby had possessed that sense of manifest destiny, of unlimited promise, which is at the heart of the myth of America. The East lacked room for that kind of innocence, for the wonder and awe which Nick imagines must have flowered in the eyes of the sailors who first saw the "fresh, green breast of the new world." The East haunts Nick. It is full of "careless people, [who] smashed up things and creatures and then retreated back into their money or their vast carelessness, or whatever it was that kept them together, and let other people clean up the mess they had made." He decides to move back home, to a place with perhaps enough room for a dreamy idealism. ❖

—Jonathan Fortescue
Harvard University

List of Characters

Daisy Buchanan (née Daisy Fay) embodies the American dream. Young, beautiful, and innocent, she speaks with a voice that "sounds like money." Jay Gatsby seduced her when she was a young southern belle, but she was too restless to wait for his return from the war. She married Tom and began a long life of strife and gaiety. Patient and yet angered by the hard drinking and womanizing of her husband, she may have affairs of her own. But her reputation is spotless until the reunion with Gatsby.

Tom Buchanan had been with Nick at Yale together but had not been a close friend. Tom is a hulking, forceful man who always maintains an air of proprietorship even when dealing with people. He had been a nationally recognized football star at college and appears to still long for the moral simplicity of the struggle on the gridiron. Fabulously wealthy for someone his age, he brought a stable of horses with him from Chicago and seems to spend his time either playing polo or having extramarital affairs.

Jordan Baker is a friend of Daisy's from their childhood and helps to engineer the affair with Gatsby. She is a professional golfer, who was accused of cheating in a tournament a couple of years before the beginning of the novel. Reckless and dishonest, she latches onto Nick as someone who is careful and truthful. Opposed to the idealism and innocence of Nick, she espouses a skepticism about the power of love and faith.

Nick Carraway is the narrator. Somewhat of a cipher, he closely identifies himself with Gatsby. The son of a prominent mercantile family in the Midwest, he was educated at Yale and came to New York to make a living in the bond business. His move east was in part due to the desire to escape a potential marriage engagement.

Jay Gatsby (né James Gatz) is the son of a farmer who distinguished himself in the war. He rises to prominence in New York but claims to be something he is not. Having made a fortune as a bootlegger, he passes himself off as a respectable owner of drugstores. His grandiose vision of himself becomes enmeshed in his love for Daisy and the fact that she represents the achievement of the American dream.

George and Myrtle Wilson are poor pawns of the wealthy who drive past their gas station. Tom used the pretext of selling a car to George in order to get close enough to seduce his wife. Myrtle has fantasies of being Tom's wife and believes his lie that Daisy refuses a divorce on the grounds that she is Catholic. George and Myrtle have dreamed of moving west, but this falls apart when George learns of his wife's affair. Somewhat ill and deranged, he tells her that she may have fooled him but not God. He tells her that "God sees everything" and then points to the advertisement of oculist Dr. T. J. Eckleburg. When Myrtle mistakes Gatsby's car for Tom's she runs out to stop it and is run over. George exacts revenge by killing Gatsby and then commits suicide.

Meyer Wolfsheim is a member of the Jewish mafia. He reputedly rigged the 1919 World Series. When Gatsby returned from the war Wolfsheim took him under his wing as a protégé. He mistakes Nick for someone interested in making a similar "business gonnegtion." ❖

Critical Views

[Maxwell E. Perkins (1884–1947) was a famous editor at Charles Scribner's Sons and worked closely with Fitzgerald, Ernest Hemingway, Thomas Wolfe, and other important American writers in revising and polishing their works for publication. In the following letter, Perkins, while admiring *The Great Gatsby*, finds Fitzgerald's characterization of the central figure a little too vague and recommends that Fitzgerald supply additional information on his background.]

I think you have every kind of right to be proud of this book. It is an extraordinary book, suggestive of all sorts of thoughts and moods. ⟨. . .⟩ I have only two actual criticisms:

One is that among a set of characters marvelously palpable and vital—I would know Tom Buchanan if I met him on the street and would avoid him—Gatsby is somewhat vague. The reader's eyes can never quite focus upon him, his outlines are dim. Now everything about Gatsby is more or less a mystery, i.e. more or less vague, and this may be somewhat of an artistic intention, but I think it is mistaken. Couldn't *he* be physically described as distinctly as the others, and couldn't you add one or two characteristics like the use of that phrase "old sport"— not verbal, but physical ones, perhaps. I think that for some reason or other a reader—this was true of Mr. Scribner and of Louise ⟨Mrs. Maxwell E. Perkins⟩—gets an idea that Gatsby is a much older man than he is, although you have the writer say that he is little older than himself. But this would be avoided if on his first appearance he was seen as vividly as Daisy and Tom are, for instance—and I do not think your scheme would be impaired if you made him so.

The other point is also about Gatsby: his career must remain mysterious, of course. But in the end you make it pretty clear that his wealth came through his connection with Wolfsheim. You also suggest this much earlier. Now almost all readers numerically are going to be puzzled by his having all this wealth and are going to feel entitled to an explanation. To give a distinct and definite one would be, of course, utterly absurd. It did occur to me, though, that you might here and there interpolate some phrases, and possibly incidents, little touches of various kinds, that would suggest that he was in some active way mysteriously engaged. You do have him called on the telephone, but couldn't he be seen once or twice consulting at his parties with people of some sort of mysterious significance, from the political, the gambling, the sporting world, or whatever it may be. I know I am floundering, but that fact may help you to see what I mean. The *total* lack of an explanation through so large a part of the story does seem to me a defect—or not of an explanation, but of the suggestion of an explanation. I wish you were here so I could talk about it to you, for then I know I could at least make you understand what I mean. What Gatsby did ought never to be definitely imparted, even if it could be. Whether he was an innocent tool in the hands of somebody else, or to what degree he was this, ought not to be explained. But if some sort of business activity of his were simply adumbrated, it would lend further probability to that part of the story.

There is one other point: in giving deliberately Gatsby's biography, when he gives it to the narrator, you do depart from the method of the narrative in some degree, for otherwise almost everything is told, and beautifully told, in the regular flow of it, in the succession of events or in accompaniment with them. But you can't avoid the biography altogether. I thought you might find ways to let the truth of some of his claims like "Oxford" and his army career come out, bit by bit, in the course of actual narrative. I mention the point anyway, for consideration in this interval before I send the proofs.

—Maxwell E. Perkins, Letter to F. Scott Fitzgerald (20 November 1924), *Editor to Author: The Letters of Maxwell E. Perkins*, ed. John Hall Wheelock (New York: Scribner's, 1950), pp. 38–40

F. Scott Fitzgerald on His Conception of Gatsby

[Fitzgerald, replying to Perkins's letter, states that the vagueness of his portrayal of Gatsby was deliberate. He goes on to say that Tom Buchanan is perhaps the best character he has ever drawn.]

Strange to say, my notion of Gatsby's vagueness was O.K. What you and Louise and Mr. Charles Scribner found wanting was that:

I myself didn't know what Gatsby looked like or was engaged in and you felt it. If I'd known and kept it from you you'd have been *too impressed with my knowledge to protest.* This is a complicated idea but I'm sure you'll understand. But I know now—and as a penalty for not having known first, in other words to make sure, I'm going to tell more.

It seems of almost mystical significance to me that you thought he was older—the man I had in mind, half-unconsciously, *was* older (a specific individual) and evidently, without so much as a definite word, I conveyed the fact. Or rather I must qualify this Shaw Desmond trash by saying that I conveyed it without a word that I can at present or for the life of me trace. (I think Shaw Desmond was one of your bad bets—I was the other.)

Anyhow after careful searching of the files (of a man's mind here) for the Fuller Magee case and after having had Zelda draw pictures until her fingers ache I know Gatsby better than I know my own child. My first instinct after your letter was to let him go and have Tom Buchanan dominate the book (I suppose he's the best character I've ever done—I think he and the brother in *Salt* and Hurstwood in *Sister Carrie* are the three best characters in American fiction in the last twenty years, perhaps and perhaps not) but Gatsby sticks in my heart. I had him for awhile, then lost him, and now I know I have him again.

—F. Scott Fitzgerald, Letter to Maxwell E. Perkins (c. 20 December 1924), *The Letters of F. Scott Fitzgerald,* ed. Andrew Turnbull (New York: Scribner's, 1963), pp. 172–73

H. L. Mencken on the Style of *The Great Gatsby*

[H. L. Mencken (1880–1950) was one of the most important essayists, critics, and book reviewers of his generation. After writing books on George Bernard Shaw and Friedrich Nietzsche early in his career, he wrote essays and reviews in many magazines, including the *Smart Set*, which he cofounded with George Jean Nathan. Many of these essays were collected in a six-volume series, *Prejudices* (1919–27). In this review of *The Great Gatsby*, Mencken finds the novel less substantial than *This Side of Paradise* but more elegantly written. Mencken also relishes its satire of American society, of which he was a relentless and at times bitter critic.]

This story is obviously unimportant, and though, as I shall show, it has its place in the Fitzgerald canon, it is certainly not to be put on the same shelf with, say, *This Side of Paradise*. What ails it, fundamentally, is the plain fact that it is simply a story—that Fitzgerald seems to be far more interested in maintaining its suspense than in getting under the skins of its people. It is not that they are false; it is that they are taken too much for granted. Only Gatsby himself genuinely lives and breathes. The rest are mere marionettes—often astonishingly lifelike, but nevertheless not quite alive.

What gives the story distinction is something quite different from the management of the action or the handling of the characters; it is the charm and beauty of the writing. In Fitzgerald's first days it seemed almost unimaginable that he would ever show such qualities. His writing, then, was extraordinarily slipshod—at times almost illiterate. He seemed to be devoid of any feeling for the color and savor of words. He could see people clearly and he could devise capital situations, but as writer qua writer he was apparently little more than a bright college boy. The critics of the Republic were not slow to discern the fact. They praised *This Side of Paradise* as a story, as a social document, but they were almost unanimous in denouncing it as a piece of writing.

It is vastly to Fitzgerald's credit that he appears to have taken their caveats seriously and pondered them to good effect. In *The Great Gatsby* the highly agreeable fruits of that pondering are visible. The story, for all its basic triviality, has a fine texture, a careful and brilliant finish. The obvious phrase is simply not in it. The sentences roll along smoothly, sparkingly, variously. There is evidence in every line of hard and intelligent effort. It is a quite new Fitzgerald who emerges from this little book and the qualities that he shows are dignified and solid. *This Side of Paradise,* after all, might have been merely a lucky accident. But *The Great Gatsby,* a far inferior story at bottom, is plainly the product of a sound and stable talent, conjured into being by hard work. ⟨. . .⟩

Thus Fitzgerald, the stylist, arises to challenge Fitzgerald, the social historian, but I doubt that the latter ever quite succumbs to the former. The thing that chiefly interests the basic Fitzgerald is still the florid show of modern American life—and especially the devil's dance that goes on at the top. He is unconcerned about the sweatings and sufferings of the nether herd; what engrosses him is the high carnival of those who have too much money to spend and too much time for the spending of it. Their idiotic pursuit of sensation, their almost incredible stupidity and triviality, their glittering swinishness— these are the things that go into his notebook.

In *The Great Gatsby,* though he does not go below the surface, he depicts this rattle and hullabaloo with great gusto and, I believe, with sharp accuracy. The Long Island he sets before us is no fanciful Alsatia; it actually exists. More, it is worth any social historian's study, for its influence upon the rest of the country is immense and profound. What is vogue among the profiteers of Manhattan and their harlots today is imitated by the flappers of the Bible Belt country clubs week after next. The whole tone of American society, once so highly formalized and so suspicious of change, is now taken largely from frail ladies who were slinging hash a year ago.

—H. L. Mencken, "As H. L. M. Sees It," *Baltimore Evening Sun,* 2 May 1925, p. 9

❖

ALFRED KAZIN ON GATSBY AND THE FAILURE OF THE AMERICAN DREAM

[Alfred Kazin (b. 1915) is one of the most distinguished critics of our time and the author of many books, including *Bright Book of Life: American Novelists and Storytellers from Hemingway to Mailer* (1973), *An American Procession* (1984), and *A Writer's America: Landscape in Literature* (1988). In this extract, taken from Kazin's important early study of American literature, *On Native Grounds* (1942), Kazin sees the character of Jay Gatsby as prototypical of the ambiance of the 1920s and also of the failure of the American dream, since Gatsby's wealth and success do not bring him the happiness he seeks.]

To have approached Gatsby from the outside would have meant a sacrifice of Gatsby himself—a knowledge of everything in Gatsby's world save Gatsby. But the tragedy here is pure confession, a supplication complete in the human note it strikes. Fitzgerald could sound the depths of Gatsby's life because he himself could not conceive any other. Out of his own weariness and fascination with damnation he caught Gatsby's damnation, caught it as only someone so profoundly attentive to Gatsby's dream could have pierced to the self-lie behind it. The book has no real scale; it does not rest on any commanding vision, nor is it in any sense a major tragedy. But it is a great flooding moment, a moment's intimation and penetration; and as Gatsby's disillusion becomes felt at the end it strikes like a chime through the mind. It was as if Fitzgerald, the playboy moving with increasing despair through this tinsel world of Gatsby's, had reached that perfect moment, before the break of darkness and death, when the mind does really and absolutely know itself—a moment when only those who have lived by Gatsby's great illusion, lived by the tinsel and the glamour, can feel the terrible force of self-betrayal. This was the playboy's rare apotheosis, and one all the more moving precisely because all of Gatsby's life was summed up in it, precisely because his decline and death gave a meaning to his life that it had not in itself possessed.

Here was the chagrin, the waste of the American success story in the twenties: here, in a story that was a moment's revelation. Yet think, Fitzgerald seems to say to us, of how little Gatsby wanted at bottom—not to understand society, but to ape it; not to compel the world, but to live in it. His own dream of wealth meant nothing in itself; he merely wanted to buy back the happiness he had lost—Daisy, now the rich man's wife—when he had gone away to war. So the great Gatsby house at West Egg glittered with all the lights of the twenties, and there were always parties, and always Gatsby's supplicating hand, reaching out to make out of glamour what he had lost by the cruelty of chance. "Gatsby believed in the green light, the orgastic future that year by year recedes before us. It eluded us then, but that's no matter—tomorrow we will run faster, stretch out our arms farther. . . . And one fine morning—" So the great Gatsby house, Gatsby having failed in his dream, now went out with all its lights, save for that last unexpected and uninvited guest whom Nick heard at the closed Gatsby door one night, the guest "who had been away at the ends of the earth and didn't know that the party was over." And now there was only the wry memory of Gatsby's dream, left in that boyhood schedule of September 12, 1906, with its promise of industry and self-development—"Rise from bed. . . . Study electricity . . . Work. . . . Practice elocution, poise and how to attain it. . . . Read one improving book or magazine per week." So all the lights of Fitzgerald's golden time went out with Jay Gatsby—Gatsby, the flower of the republic, the bootlegger who made the American dream his own, and died by it. "So we beat on, boats against the current, borne back ceaselessly into the past."

—Alfred Kazin, *On Native Grounds: An Interpretation of Modern American Literature* (New York: Reynal & Hitchcock, 1942), pp. 321–22

MAXWELL GEISMAR ON GATSBY AS A PROLETARIAN CHARACTER

[Maxwell Geismar (1909–1979) was a leading American critic and biographer. Among his books are *American Moderns, from Rebellion to Conformity* (1958), *Henry James and the Jacobites* (1963), and *Mark Twain: An American Prophet* (1970). In this extract, Geismar believes Fitzgerald to have conceived Gatsby as almost a proletarian character in that he comes from a small town in North Dakota and is not "cultivated" as many of Fitzgerald's upper-class characters are.]

⟨. . .⟩ notice that Gatsby is also a new *social* character—one who has no proper education and not the slightest pretense to breeding, who never grew up in Geneva and never went to Yale; whose only clubs are 'trade associations,' whose clothes are primary rather than pastel, and whose method of conversational approach ranges from 'chum' to 'old chap.' Gatsby is diametrically opposed to all of Fitzgerald's handsome, luxurious, and cultivated young men, and the first of the major figures to flaunt such handicaps. For F. Scott Fitzgerald, in fact, for this prime Muse of the Jazz Age, James Gatz of North Dakota—granting the inevitable exception of his millions—is almost the equivalent of a proletarian protagonist. Yet, as the Great Gatsby, he is more than a class symbol. He is a sort of cultural hero, and the story of Gatsby's illusion is the story of an age's illusion, too. The bare outlines of his career—the upward struggle from poverty and ignorance; the naïve aspirations toward refinement and the primal, ruthless energy of these aspirations; the fixation of this provincial soul upon a childlike notion of beauty and grace and the reliance upon material power as the single method of satisfying his searching and inarticulate spirit—these are surely the elements of a dominant cultural legend in its purest, most sympathetic form. And through a consummate choice of detail Fitzgerald has made the legend live. Gauche, ridiculous, and touching as James Gatz is, he is surely our native adolescent, raised on the western reverberations of Vanderbilt and Gould, entering a new world full of shining secrets 'that only Midas and Morgan and Maecenas knew'—a barefoot boy in the land of steel, and even, in a rather deeper sense, a cousin, say, of Huck Finn, but now drifting in the eddies and backwaters of the Long Island Sound. Whatever there is of permanence in *The Great Gatsby* derives from the fact that here, by one of those fortunate coincidences which form the record of artistic achievement, the deepest inner convictions of the writer have met with and matched those of his time and place. The 'illusive rhythm, the fragment of lost words' that Nick Carraway tries to recall are the rhythm and words of an American myth. 'But they made no sound, and what I had almost remembered was uncommunicable forever.'

—Maxwell Geismar, "F. Scott Fitzgerald: Orestes at the Ritz," *The Last of the Provincials: The American Novel 1915–1925* (Boston: Houghton Mifflin, 1947), pp. 319–20

EDWIN S. FUSSELL ON *THE GREAT GATSBY* AS AN INDICTMENT OF THE AMERICAN QUEST FOR YOUTH

[Edwin S. Fussell (b. 1922), a former professor of English at the University of California at San Diego–La Jolla, is the author of many books of criticism, including *Frontier: American Literature and the American West* (1965) and *The French Side of Henry James* (1990). In this extract, Fussell studies Gatsby's attitude toward youth and sees it as prototypical of the American desire for youth and freedom from the constraints of history.]

Gatsby, we are told, was "overwhelmingly aware of the *youth* and mystery that *wealth* imprisons and *preserves,* of the freshness of many clothes, and of Daisy, gleaming like silver, safe and proud above the hot struggle of the poor" (my italics). Her voice is frequently mentioned as mysteriously enchanting—it is the typifying feature of her role as *la belle dame sans merci—* and throughout the action it serves to suggest her loveliness and desirability. But only Gatsby, in a rare moment of vision, is able to make explicit the reasons for its subtle and elusive

33

magic: "It was full of money—that was the inexhaustible charm that rose and fell in it, the jingle of it, the cymbals' song of it. . . . High in a white palace the king's daughter, the golden girl. . . ."

Possession of an image like Daisy is all that Gatsby can finally conceive as "success"; and Gatsby is meant to be a very representative American in the intensity of his yearning for success, as well as in the symbols which he equates with it. Gatsby performs contemporary variations on an old American pattern, the rags-to-riches story exalted by American legend as early as Crevecoeur's *Letters from an American Farmer*. But the saga is primarily that of a legendary Benjamin Franklin, whose celebrated youthful resolutions are parodied in those that the adolescent Gatsby wrote on the back flyleaf of his copy of *Hopalong Cassidy*. As an indictment of American philistinism, Fitzgerald's burlesque is spare and sharp; what accounts for its impression of depth is Fitzgerald's fictionally realized perception that Gatsby's was not a unique, but a pervasive American social pattern. Grounding his parody in Franklin's *Autobiography* gave Fitzgerald's critique a historical density and a breadth of implication that one associates only with major fiction.

The connection between Gatsby's individual tragedy and the tragedy of his whole civilization is also made (and again, through symbol) with respect to historical attitudes. Gatsby's relation to history is summed up in his devotion to the green light that burns on Daisy's dock. When Nick first sees Gatsby, he is in an attitude of supplication, a gesture that pathetically travesties the gestures of worship; Nick finally observes that the object of his trembling piety is this green light which, until his disillusion, is one of Gatsby's "enchanted objects." In the novel's concluding passage, toward which all action and symbol is relentlessly tending, one is given finally the full implications of the green light as symbol ("Gatsby believed in the green light, the orgastic future").

Gatsby, with no historical sense whatsoever, is the fictional counterpart of that American philistine maxim that "history is bunk"; and he may recall, too, for those interested in such comparisons, the more crowing moods of Emerson and Thoreau, and the "timelessness" of their visions and exhortations. But for Fitzgerald, this contemptuous repudiation of tradition, historical necessity, and moral determinism, however un-self-conscious, was deluded and hubristic. When he finally came to see, as he did in *Gatsby,* that in this irresponsibility lay the real meaning behind the American obsession with youth, he was able to know Gatsby as a miserable, twentieth century Ponce de León. And his fictional world was no longer simply the Jazz Age, the Lost Generation, but the whole of American civilization as it culminated in his own time.

—Edwin S. Fussell, "Fitzgerald's Brave New World," *ELH* 19, No. 4 (December 1952): 296–97

A. E. DYSON ON GATSBY'S FAITH

[A. E. Dyson (b. 1928) is a distinguished British critic and author of *The Crazy Fabric: Essays in Irony* (1965) and, with Julian Lovelock, *Masterful Images: English Poetry from Metaphysicals to Romantics* (1976). He is a former Senior Lecturer in English and American Studies at the University of East Anglia. In this extract, Dyson notes that what distinguishes Gatsby from the other characters in the book is his "faith"—the fact that he believes in himself and in his illusions—but this very faith fails when it is put to the test in the real world.]

In one sense Gatsby is the apotheosis of his rootless society. His background is cosmopolitan, his past a mystery, his temperament that of an opportunist entirely oblivious to the claims of people or the world outside. His threadbare self-dramatisation, unremitting selfishness, and attempts to make something out of nothing are the same in kind as those of the waste-land society, and different only in intensity. Yet this intensity springs from a quality which he alone has: and this we might call "faith." He really believes in himself and his illusions: and this quality of faith, however grotesque it must seem with such an object, sets him apart from the cynically armoured midgets whom he epitomizes. It makes him bigger than they are, and more vulnerable. It is, also, a quality which commands respect from Carraway: since at the very least, "faith" protects Gatsby from the evasiveness, the conscious hypocrisy of the Toms and Daisies of the world, conferring something of the heroic on what he does; and at the best it might still turn out to be the "way in" to some kind of reality beyond the romantic facade, the romantic alchemy which, despite his cynicism, Carraway still half hopes one day to find. ⟨. . .⟩

As Carraway comes to know Gatsby, he wavers between scepticism and faith. He sees, clearly, in Gatsby the faults which he scorns in others—"charm" that is simply a technique for success, self-centredness masquerading as heroic vision, romantic pretensions based on economic corruption and a total disregard for humanity—yet he is impressed, despite himself, by the faith which transmutes all this into another pattern. Gatsby is different from the others in that he means every word he says, really believes in the uniqueness of his destiny. His romantic clichés, unlike those of Tom or Daisy, are used with simple belief that they are his own discovery, his own prerogative, his own guarantee of Olympian apartness and election. He is "trying to forget something very sad that happened . . . long ago." He has "tried very hard to die but seemed to bear an enchanted life." To listen to him is like "skimming hastily through a dozen magazines"—and yet is not like that at all, since Gatsby's faith really has brought the dead clichés back to life again, or at any rate to some semblance of life. So much in his account that might have been empty boasting turns out to be true. He has been to Oxford—after a fashion. His credentials from the commissioner of police for whom he was "able to do . . . a favour once" are genuine—they prevent him from being arrested for breaking a traffic law. His love for Daisy, too, is real, up to a point: there is a moment when it seems that he has achieved the impossible, and actually realized his fantastic programme for returning to the past.

The tragedy—for it is a tragic novel, though of an unorthodox kind—lies in the fact that Gatsby can go only so far and no further. Faith can still remove sizeable molehills, but is absolutely powerless when it comes to mountains. The ultimate romantic affirmation, "I'll always love you alone" cannot be brought to life: certainly not in the waste land; not when people like Daisy, and Gatsby himself, are involved. Gatsby's faith has to break, in the end, against a reality radically incompatible with it. But in so breaking, it makes him a tragic figure: and unites him symbolically with many men more worthy than himself—with, indeed, the general lot of mankind.

—A. E. Dyson, *"The Great Gatsby:* Thirty-six Years After," *Modern Fiction Studies* 7, No. 1 (Spring 1961): 42–44

BRIAN WAY ON GATSBY'S HEROISM

[Brian Way is a former Senior Lecturer in English at University College in Swansea, England. He has written *Development through Drama* (1967) and *F. Scott Fitzgerald and the Art of Social Fiction* (1980). In this extract, Way believes Gatsby to be a heroic character in his attempt to preserve and live by his illusions, even though the objects of those illusions—particularly Daisy Buchanan—were unworthy of them.]

The core of Gatsby's tragedy is not only that he lived by dreams, but that the woman and the class and the way of life of which he dreamed—that life of the rich which the novel so ruthlessly exposes—fell so far short of the scope of his imagination. Daisy is a trivial, callous, cowardly woman who may dream a little herself but who will not let her dreams, or such unpleasant realities as running over Myrtle Wilson, disturb her comfort. That Gatsby should have dreamt of her, given his marvellous parties for her, is the special edge to his fate. Fitzgerald conveys the intolerable bitterness of this situation with the sureness of touch that never fails him in this novel. He shows Gatsby watching over Daisy from the grounds of her house, the night after the accident, imagining that she might still come to him, and that he is protecting her from her brutal husband. Meanwhile, Tom and Daisy are sitting comfortably in their kitchen over fried chicken and bottled ale, coming to a comfortable working arrangement for their future lives. There is a banal and shabby intimacy about their marriage, it is a realistic, if worthless, practical arrangement that suits their shallow personalities. Outside, in the night, stands Gatsby, the man of tremendous and unconquerable illusions, "watching over nothing". There is a final postscript on the Buchanans when Nick meets Tom in New York, into which Fitzgerald concentrates more bitterness about the rich than he expressed anywhere outside *Tender Is the Night*—

> They were careless people, Tom and Daisy—they smashed up things and creatures and then retreated back into their money or their vast carelessness, or whatever it was that kept them together, and let other people clear up the mess they had made. . . .

By the close of the novel, Fitzgerald has completed his immensely difficult task of convincing us that Gatsby's capacity for illusion is poignant and heroic, in spite of the banality of his aspirations and the worthlessness of the objects of his dreams. The poignancy is in such touches as the car which drives up to Gatsby's long after Gatsby is dead: "Probably it was some final guest, who had been away at the ends of the earth and didn't know that the party was over." The heroic quality is there in his vigil in the garden, in the scale of his entertainments, the determination behind his criminality. In the closing passage there is a sudden enlargement of the theme—a vision of America as the continent of lost innocence and lost illusions. The Dutch sailors who first came to Long Island had an unspoilt continent before them, something "commensurate with their capacity for wonder". Fitzgerald's greatness was to have retained a sense of wonder as deep as the sailors' on that first landfall. His tragedy was to have had, not a continent to wonder at, but only the green light at the end of Daisy's dock, and the triviality of Daisy herself. The evolution of such triviality was his particular tragedy, and the tragedy of America.

—Brian Way, "Scott Fitzgerald," *New Left Review* No. 21 (October 1963): 43–44

[James E. Miller, Jr. (b. 1920) is a former professor of
English at the University of Chicago and author of many
books, including *Start with the Sun: Studies in Cosmic
Poetry* (1960), *Walt Whitman* (1962; rev. 1990), and
The American Quest for a Supreme Fiction (1979). In
this extract, from *F. Scott Fitzgerald: His Art and His
Technique* (1964), Miller studies the short story
"Absolution," originally intended as a prologue to *The
Great Gatsby,* and finds in it an anticipation of a tech-
nique that Miller terms "magic suggestiveness."]

"Absolution" is of interest not only because of its intrinsic merit
as a short story but also because it was first written as a prologue to *The Great Gatsby.* It achieves something of the com-
pact structure of the novel by its use of a frame: the story
opens with an eleven-year-old boy, Rudolph Miller, visiting a
priest, Father Schwartz, to confess a "terrible sin" (twice he had
told a lie in the confessional). After Rudolph begins to relate his
sin in somewhat incoherent language, there is a break in the
text and his story is continued in the third person; in the final
scene, the boy has just finished telling what he has done and is
awaiting the reaction of the priest. The materials for the frame
come from a splitting of the final episode of the narrative; the
previous events are placed between the two halves. Since the
transition in Rudolph, with which the story is primarily con-
cerned, is achieved in this final episode, the frame is an integral
part of the story. Such a rearrangement of the chronology does
more, however, than give form and unity. The opening scene
permits the representation of the priest's thoughts at the opening of the story before Rudolph is introduced: this initial characterization of the man who listens to Rudolph's tale colors all the
following incidents related from Rudolph's point of view and
establishes the probability of the confirmation of Rudolph's
"own inner convictions."

In "Absolution," Fitzgerald has apparently attempted and
perhaps achieved the art of "magic suggestiveness." He has
focused attention on Rudolph's visit to the priest, an incident

which, because it portrays a crucial change in the boy, suggests much more than is explicitly stated about Rudolph's character and future. After he has finished relating his "terrible sin," Rudolph listens to the priest mutter incoherently of "things going glimmering" and of a glittering fair, which "will just hang out there in the night like a colored balloon—like a big yellow lantern on a pole." Rudolph somehow understands:

> . . . underneath his terror he felt that his own inner convictions were confirmed. There was something ineffably gorgeous somewhere that had nothing to do with God. He no longer thought that God was angry at him about the original lie, because He must have understood that Rudolph had done it to make things finer in the confessional, brightening up the dinginess of his admissions by saying a thing radiant and proud. At the moment when he had affirmed immaculate honor a silver pennon had flapped out into the breeze somewhere and there had been the crunch of leather and the shine of silver spurs and a troop of horsemen waiting for a dawn on a low green hill.

This strange vision, perhaps a child's version of the Gatsby dream, seems to have developed from a glimmering abstraction into a concrete image, and not far from the surface there seems to be a sensual or even sexual motivation. The Swede girls, whose laughter at the opening of the story made Father Schwartz "pray aloud for the twilight to come," reappear at the end of the story in a brilliant vignette:

> Outside the window the blue sirocco trembled over the wheat, and girls with yellow hair walked sensuously along roads that bounded the fields, calling innocent, exciting things to the young men who were working in the lines between the grain. Legs were shaped under starchless gingham, and rims of the necks of dresses were warm and damp. For five hours now hot fertile life had burned in the afternoon. It would be night in three hours, and all along the land there would be these blonde Northern girls and the tall young men from the farms lying out beside the wheat, under the moon.

This tableau, charged throughout with sexual suggestion, serves as a backdrop to point up dramatically the incoherent frustrations of the old Catholic priest, celibate by profession, and the inchoate awakening of the eleven-year-old boy, just emerging on "the lonely secret road of adolescence."

Though discarded as a prologue to *The Great Gatsby*, "Absolution" does serve as a prologue to Fitzgerald's new technique, his art of "magic suggestiveness." As Carl Van Vechten said in reviewing *The Great Gatsby*, "When I read Absolution in the *American Mercury* I realized that there were many potential qualities inherent in Scott Fitzgerald which hitherto had not been too apparent." These potentialities were realized magnificently in *The Great Gatsby*.

—James E. Miller, Jr., *F. Scott Fitzgerald: His Art and His Technique* (New York: New York University Press, 1964), pp. 103–5

JOAN M. ALLEN ON GATSBY AS A CHRIST FIGURE

[Joan M. Allen (b. 1938) is the author of *Candles and Carnival Lights: The Catholic Sensibility of F. Scott Fitzgerald* (1978), from which this extract is taken. Here, Allen examines Gatsby's real father and his foster father (Dan Cody), finding them both examples of "failed paternity" and seeing in Gatsby's death a parallel to the death of Jesus Christ.]

Neither Gatsby's natural or spiritual father has been able to provide him with values or a vision worthy of his spirit. Mr. Gatz is essentially a good man, he is conventionally virtuous, but even though he subscribes to the American formula for success, he has neither the talent nor temperament to make his way. We have seen that the young Gatsby's appeal to a spiritual father merely strengthened his notion that religion offered nothing to nourish him. At seventeen James Gatz forever rejected his natural parents—"his imagination had never really accepted them as his parents at all"—and created the persona Jay Gatsby as he rowed out to Dan Cody's yacht. For over a year Gatz had lived an itinerant existence along the shore of the lake, his heart in a constant turbulent riot, haunted by visions of "ineffable gaudiness," the corruption of the "something ineffably gorgeous somewhere that had nothing to do with God" which Rudolph Miller had been convinced existed for him. In his nightly dreams, the victim of his own romantic readiness, Gatz sees the "promise that the rock of the world was founded securely on a fairy's wing."

When he meets Dan Cody, Jay Gatsby springs full-blown from his platonic conception of himself, "a son of God" fit to "be about his Father's business, the service of a vast, vulgar, and meretricious beauty." But this is a Trimalchio, not a Christ, and the God he worships is Mammon. Gatsby's foster father, Dan Cody, is a self-made millionaire from transactions in Montana copper, a pioneer debauchee who had transported to the East the violence of the frontier brothel and saloon. His name is the amalgam of Daniel Boone, the pioneer, and William Cody, the buffalo slaughterer and charlatan carnival man, which makes him an apt guide through the tawdry carnival which Father Schwartz had cautioned Rudolph to avoid. Cody is, in effect, John the Baptist to this "Son of God," for Cody has been preaching the materialistic word and passes on the mantle to this false messiah who will carry it to his tragic end. During his time with Cody, Gatsby learns not to drink, for the foolish Cody, who was vulnerable when drinking, had been victimized by women as Chevalier O'Keefe had been. An especially bitter lesson for him evolves out of Dan Cody's $25,000 legacy of which he was cheated by Cody's last female companion. He is never to be a man of inherited wealth, so he sets about His Father's business, amassing a fortune by any means. Three fathers had failed Gatsby, and even Nick, who scolds him for his rudeness before his first meeting with Daisy and who acts as his father-confessor, fails to save him.

When Gatsby lies dead amidst the ineffable gaudiness of his earth-bound vision, his natural father arrives from the West to witness his end. Certain ironic parallels between the figures of Christ and Gatsby are unmistakable, and the description of Gatsby's death and burial is a striking example of Fitzgerald's use of elements of the Christian myth in telling the story of his bogus Christ. Gatsby's gratuitous sacrifice for Daisy, like Christ's for mankind, is the direct cause of his violent death; but this travesty of Christ is scourged by his profound disappointment rather than by Roman soldiers as the death scene approaches, for Nick conjectures that Gatsby must have felt a sharp sense of loss and futility for having lived too long with a single dream. Refusing help, Gatsby carries to his pool a pneumatic mattress which will bear the burden of his dead body. At noon George Wilson is seen on Gad's [God's] Hill, and the murder will occur at about three in the afternoon, the hour of Christ's death. Like Christ, Gatsby is left among strangers during a three-day vigil, and "On the third day" his true identity is resurrected with the telegram of Henry C. Gatz of Minnesota. When he arrives to reclaim his son, he reveals the meager quality of his parentage in his pride at Gatsby's affluence, which overwhelms his grief, and in his statement to Nick that if Gatsby had lived, he would have been a great man like James J. Hill. Just as surely as God sent His son to die for a dream, so Henry Gatz, years before, had set into motion his son's destruction. Gatz had been a derelict earthly father; his worship of materialism, the substance of his earthbound dream for his son, is an ironic analogue to God's purpose for his son.

—Joan M. Allen, *Candles and Carnival Lights: The Catholic Sensibility of F. Scott Fitzgerald* (New York: New York University Press, 1978), pp. 108–9

JUDITH FETTERLEY ON THE CHARACTER OF DAISY

[Judith Fetterley (b. 1938) is a professor of English at the State University of New York at Albany. She has edited *Provisions: A Reader from 18th-Century American Women* (1985) and Alice Cary's *Clovernook Sketches and Other Stories* (1987) and written *The Resisting Reader: A Feminist Approach to American Fiction* (1978), from which the following extract is taken. Here, Fetterley finds that Daisy Buchanan is not merely the object of Gatsby's desires but essential to Gatsby's own self-image and self-esteem.]

But Daisy does not simply represent or incarnate that magical world Gatsby desires; she is herself the ultimate object in it. It is she for whom men compete, and possessing her is the clearest sign that one has made it into that magical world. Gatsby's desire for Daisy is enhanced by the fact that she is the object of the desires of so many other men: "It excited him, too, that many men had already loved Daisy—it increased her value in his eyes." Their desire ratifies his sense of her symbolic significance. That Daisy is the most expensive item on the market is a point Tom makes when he gives her on the night before they are married a string of pearls valued at $350,000. Daisy is that which money exists to buy; her presence both indicates the fact of money and gives point to its possession. Having her makes Tom Buchanan's house in East Egg finished and "right"; not having her makes Gatsby's mansion in West Egg incomplete and "wrong." It is not surprising, then, that Daisy's meaning should crystallize for Gatsby, and for Nick, around the perception that her voice is full of money. One can only wonder that it took them so long to formulate the obvious.

But money is never just money to the imagination that made a fetish of being rich: "that was the inexhaustible charm that rose and fell in it, the jingle of it, the cymbals' song of it. . . . High in a white palace the king's daughter, the golden girl." Money is coin of the realm of romance, and the golden girl is valued not just because she provides access to the king's palace or because she is expensive. She is valued as well for the connotations that shimmer in the words "high" and "white"—a rarefied kingdom, pure and free, where the imagination reigns unsullied by the ashy wasteland of the real world and romps like the mind of God. The high white palace is an analogue for Gatsby's "secret place above the trees," from which he can look down on the world and "suck on the pap of life, gulp down the incomparable milk of wonder"; and Daisy herself becomes, as the metaphors suggest, the symbol of the possibilities for wonder that his imagination creates.

The pervasive spatial metaphor, however, reveals another aspect of the golden girl crucial to her hold on the impersonality of the romantic imagination. She is hard to get; she has to be worked for, dragons must be fought, castles penetrated, and walls scaled. And the harder she is to get the more she is valued, because the quest for and possession of her gives the pink-suited knight his identity. When Gatsby weds "his unutterable visions" to Daisy's "perishable breath" and makes her his holy grail, she becomes the organizing point of his existence, providing him with a structure that determines what he will do and who he will be. She becomes his access to a certain self-image: "he wanted to recover something, some idea of himself perhaps, that had gone into loving Daisy." It is through Daisy that Gatsby acquires the image of himself as the faithful unto death, the one for whom time and change mean nothing, whose love is pure flame that feeds upon and fires itself. It is through her that he realizes himself in the posture of the dedicated lover who reads a Chicago newspaper for five years in the hope simply of catching a glimpse of her name. It is for her that he accomplishes the heroic feat of making himself into a millionaire, and it is for her that he builds his palace in West Egg.

This investment of self in Daisy means, of course, that Gatsby needs Daisy to validate him. Since everything is done for her, she must be worthy of this investment in her and she must provide a response commensurate to it. The ritual of validation is the last of the symbolic functions Daisy performs for Gatsby. Gatsby will have his great reunion with Daisy only at his house or, if that is impossible, then next door to it, for he does not wish to see *her* but rather for her to see what he has done *for* her, as if only through her eyes will his vision of himself be made real. The same implicit demand is there when he spills out before her his wealth of gorgeous shirts: they are deployed to exact tribute from her. It is no wonder that Daisy cries. What response could possibly be adequate to this demonstration? Her tears are an understandable reaction at once to the pathos in the demonstration and to the pressure on her to be valuable enough to validate the identity so painfully set before her.

—Judith Fetterley, "*The Great Gatsby:* Fitzgerald's *droit de seigneur,*" *The Resisting Reader: A Feminist Approach to American Fiction* (Bloomington: Indiana University Press, 1978), pp. 75–77

BRUCE MICHELSON ON THE MYTHIC DIMENSIONS OF *THE GREAT GATSBY*

[Bruce Michelson (b. 1948) is a professor of English at the University of Illinois and the author of *Wilbur's Poetry: Music in a Scattering Time* (1991). In this extract, Michelson examines *The Great Gatsby* as a modern adaptation of the Greek myth of Phaeton, the son of Apollo who attempts to ride in his father's golden chariot but is hurled to his death because he is unable to control the mighty horses as they go across the heavens.]

As it happens, *The Great Gatsby*'s image patterns and even the workings of its plot show more than a general family resemblance to classical tales of flying men. The legend of Phaeton is the one which echoes in this novel most persistently and strongly—so strongly that there is cause for wondering whether Phaeton isn't as deliberately called up here as Odysseus is in Leopold Bloom's wanderings around Dublin. ⟨. . .⟩

To summarize the Phaeton story as Ovid tells it: a true son of a god, young Phaeton lives in a land of mortals far to the west of Apollo's palace. Nobody takes the young man seriously when he speaks of his noble birth, and so when he has grown up strong and reckless, Phaeton journeys to the east edge of the world, the blazing home of the divine horseman, the golden palace which Ovid describes with such flourish. From one of the many "trots" to *The Metamorphoses* available in 1916:

> The palace of the Sun stood high on lofty columns, bright with glittering gold and bronze that shone like fire. Gleaming ivory crowned the gables above: the double folding doors were radiant with burnished silver. And the workmanship was more beautiful than the material. For upon the doors Mulciber had carved in relief the waters that enfold the central earth, the circle of the lands and the sky that overhangs the lands. The sea holds the dark-hued gods: tuneful Triton, changeful Proteus, and Aegaeon. . . .

And so on through many more radiant furnishings. When Phaeton arrives on high, his remorseful father hastily swears by the Styx to give the boy anything he desires; and Phaeton claims the sun and the golden chariot for one day. Apollo warns the boy of the power of the wild winged steeds, the perils of the course through the sky, the dangers of his cargo, the twistings, turnings, and grotesqueness of the path that seems so easy and perfect from below. But Phaeton is unshakable. Dawn on the fatal day throws open "her purple gates, and her courts glowing with rosy light," and Phaeton mounts to the god's place in the golden car. The young usurper manages things for a while, but soon the great horses are out of control, racing, swerving from the path, and setting the world ablaze:

> The earth bursts into flame, the highest parts first, and splits into deep cracks, and its moisture is all dried up. The meadows are burned to white ashes; the trees are consumed, green leaves and all, and the ripe grain furnishes fuel for its own destruction. But these are small losses which I am lamenting. Great cities perish with their walls, and the vast conflagration reduces whole nations to ashes.

The earth cries to heaven for mercy; with Apollo's consent, Zeus hurls his thunderbolt; and Phaeton, afire, streaks down through the air like a falling star. His body falls into the Eridanus, the river no living man has ever seen; and his sisters, grieving at his tomb, are subsequently transformed into poplars, forever dropping their amber tears into the water. Ovid's epitaph for Phaeton:

> Hic situs est Phaethon currus auriga paterni
> Quem si non tenuit magnis tamen excidit ausis.

Here lies Phaeton, who drove his father's golden car. He failed greatly, but still more greatly did he dare. Ovid begs the question: did Phaeton turn out all right in the end? Was he a true son of the god, or just a "poor son of a bitch"? As one of Ovid's flashiest tales, Phaeton's fall offers perfect raw material for making a modern hero. Here is a true mortal with his sublime and preposterous dreams, one who would risk everything for a simple "golden moment"—and as soon as he has what he wants, his world burns (literally, in this case) to ashes before his eyes. The story lives precisely because it has at its heart the paradox which haunts all the great myths of mortals who strive with gods: it appeals to our most fabulous dreams even as it cautions us to leave those dreams alone.

The golden car, the disastrous careening ride through the ash-strewn world—the general likenesses of Gatsby's story to Phaeton's fall will be immediately clear to anyone thinking of *The Great Gatsby* with Ovid in mind. But all the plot borrowings in the world could not make a modern Phaeton of Gatsby, could not make his story a living myth, were it not for Nick, a storyteller with a genuine capacity for wonder. The raw bones of a myth might be waiting for him in West Egg, just as the older tale waited centuries for Ovid; but Nick, like Ovid before him, proves the true mythmaker. Nick finds the details and the language to perform the magic, to suspend us, as he himself is suspended, somewhere between wonder and scorn for the hero of his tale, to enchant us with the very spirit that the story builds its tragedy around. The myth of Gatsby is a myth made as much of small moments and well-chosen words as it is of grand gestures, and with these small shadings we must especially concern ourselves.

> —Bruce Michelson, "The Myth of Gatsby," *Modern Fiction Studies* 26, No. 4 (Winter 1980–81): 566–68

GEORGE GARRETT ON *THE GREAT GATSBY* AS A TRIUMPH OF THE AMERICAN VERNACULAR

[George Garrett (b. 1929) is a distinguished poet, critic, and author of such historical novels as *Death of the Fox* (1971) and *The Succession* (1983). He has written a critical study of Mary Lee Settle (1988) and teaches English at the University of Virginia. In this extract, Garrett sees *The Great Gatsby* as brilliantly exemplifying the American idiom in its contrast between the written and spoken vernacular.]

Gatsby is a marvelous experiment, a triumph of the *written* American vernacular, the range, suppleness, and eloquence of it. But for the written vernacular language of the times to be fully explored, it was necessary to set it in direct contrast to the spoken language, not only in the contrast between credible dialogue in the dramatic scenes, but, occasionally and within limits, in the narration itself; thus "out of that tangle back home" and "I think he'd tanked up a good deal at luncheon. . . ." In other words, the written narration, this *book* by Nick Carraway, has to touch, however briefly, on the level of spoken narration in order to define itself clearly. Moreover, this capability is necessary if full use is to be made of the spoken vernacular in dramatic and satirical scenes. The overall effect, the created language of this book, Nick Carraway's language, offers up a full range between lyrical evocation and depths of feeling at one end and casual, if hard-knuckled, matters of fact. It allows for the poetry of intense perception to live simultaneously and at ease with a hard-edged, implacable vulgarity. Each draws strength from the conflict with the other.

This same tension of time and language is at the center of Carraway's point of view and is expressed early on in Chapter 2 as Carraway, drunk, imagines himself as a stranger capable of including even Carraway as an object in his speculative vision: "Yet high over the city our line of yellow windows must have contributed their share of human secrecy to the casual watcher in the darkening streets, and I was him too, looking up and wondering. I was within and without, simultaneously enchanted and repelled by the inexhaustible variety of life." *I was within and without. . . .* *Gatsby* becomes an intricate demonstration of that kind of complex double vision, of the *process* of it. We are not far into the story (Chapter 3) before we discover that the "book" Nick Carraway mentioned at the outset, the book that, completed, will turn out to be *The Great Gatsby,* is not yet finished, is in the process of being written. "Reading over what I have written so far, I see I have given the impression that the events of three nights several weeks apart were all that absorbed me." This additional sense of time (narrator pauses to reread what he has written so far) almost, not quite, allows for another kind of time level—the time of revision. At least it asserts that what is being reported has been carefully thought about and can be corrected if need be. And at the least, it makes the time of the composition of the story closely parallel to the reader's left-to-right, chronological adventure.

A bit later, in a number of ways, we are encouraged to *participate* actively in the narrative process, as, for example in

Chapter six, where Carraway explains and defends a narrative choice:

> He told me all this very much later, but I've put it down here with the idea of exploding those first wild rumors about his antecedents, which weren't even faintly true. Moreover he told it to me at a time of confusion, when I had reached the point of believing everything and nothing about him. So I take advantage of this short halt, while Gatsby, so to speak, caught his breath, to clear this set of misconceptions away.

Here the focus is so clearly on the process of making and of the free, if pragmatic, choices involved that the reader is strongly reminded of the story as artifact, although, ironically, it is Carraway's selective virtuosity that at once supersedes and disguises Fitzgerald's.

> —George Garrett, "Fire and Freshness: A Matter of Style in *The Great Gatsby*," *New Essays on* The Great Gatsby, ed. Matthew J. Bruccoli (Cambridge: Cambridge University Press, 1985), pp. 111–12

SARAH BEEBE FRYER ON DAISY AS A ROMANTIC CHARACTER

[Sarah Beebe Fryer (b. 1950) is the author of *Fitzgerald's New Women: Harbingers of Change* (1988), from which the following extract is taken. Here, Fryer attempts to refute the standard view that Daisy is a crass and shallow character by showing that she has romantic visions and emotional depth just as Gatsby does.]

From the opening of the novel, Fitzgerald demonstrates that Daisy, like Gatsby, is at least in part a romantic. The first clue that Daisy remembers Gatsby with more than just a passing interest appears during Nick's first visit to the Buchanans' home. Jordan tells Nick that she knows a man named Gatsby in West Egg, and Daisy, alert to an old lover's name despite five years of separation, her marriage to another man, and the birth of a daughter, suddenly interrupts: "'Gatsby?' demanded Daisy. 'What Gatsby?'" Because dinner is announced, Daisy doesn't get an immediate answer, and her question may seem insignificant to a casual reader. But later in the novel, as Jordan tells Nick of Daisy and Gatsby's early romance, we learn that Daisy cared enough about hearing Gatsby's name that evening to wake Jordan up—after she had retired early to rest before a tournament—to get news of Gatsby. This incident in and of itself does not prove that Daisy's love for Gatsby approaches his for her, but, coupled with the events that follow, it certainly suggests that she, like Gatsby, cultivates fond memories of a dream lover.

Severe tension pervades the Buchanan home as Nick dines with Jordan, Tom, and Daisy. Even before Nick learns that "Tom's got some woman in New York," his observations of the interplay between Daisy and Tom reflect the animosity between them. Their exchanges seem playful at first. Daisy accuses Tom of hurting her finger, then childishly calls him "hulking" repeatedly, since she knows it upsets him. But gradually their feud escalates. The telephone's reminders of Tom's sexual infidelity contribute to Daisy's flirtatious behavior towards Nick at the dinner table. When Tom is first called away to the telephone, Daisy affects indifference by "enthusiastically" recounting a funny story to Nick. And when the phone calls Tom away again only a few moments later, Nick observes: "As if his absence quickened something within her, Daisy leaned forward again, her voice glowing and singing."

Certainly Nick perceives that Daisy is reacting emotionally to an emotional situation, but her response is not immediately directed towards the source of her tension. Daisy responds to tension with energy, but, instead of openly confronting Tom with her anger, she enthusiastically engages herself with Nick and needles Tom through ironic remarks. Characteristically, she subjugates her desire to assert herself to her need for security. But the simple fact that she is anxious in the face of evidence of Tom's infidelity suggests that she has an emotional investment in her relationship with him. A woman who felt less would react less.

Daisy displays her intelligence, sensitivity, and suffering as she gets even with Tom throughout the evening. When Tom criticizes Jordan's family for letting her "'run around the country,'" Daisy says, "'She's going to spend lots of week-ends out here this summer. I think the home influence will be very good for her.'" Tom shows his recognition of her implications as he stares at her in silence. And Daisy continues to annoy him by making his concern about racial purity the butt of a nasty joke.

> "Did you give Nick a little heart-to-heart talk on the veranda?" demanded Tom suddenly.
>
> "Did I? . . . I can't seem to remember, but I think we talked about the Nordic race. Yes, I'm sure we did. It sort of crept up on us and the first thing you know—"

Tom interrupts Daisy and addresses Nick, thus demonstrating his recognition of—and disregard for—Daisy's covert hostility.

By this point, of course, Daisy has had a little "heart-to-heart talk" with Nick, and in it she has disclosed that she is vulnerable to emotions, and that she has been deeply—perhaps irreparably—hurt. When Nick, having recognized "that turbulent emotions possessed her," asks Daisy about her daughter, Daisy cautiously exposes her feelings to him through her account of the child's birth:

> "Well, she was less than an hour old and Tom was God knows where. I woke up out of the ether with an utterly abandoned feeling, and asked the nurse right away if it was a boy or a girl. She told me it was a girl, and so I turned my head away and wept. 'All right,' I said, 'I'm glad it's a girl. And I hope she'll be a fool—that is the best thing a girl can be in this world, a beautiful little fool.'"

Daisy's story about the child's birth reveals a lot about her own unhappiness. She would choose to be a fool—to be incapable of and invulnerable to ideas and emotions—if she could; but the foundation of her desire to be unfeeling is experience: she does feel, she has suffered, and her desire for her daughter to be a "fool" is actually a desire to shelter her from experiencing the pain that Daisy herself has known. Daisy's remarks about the child's birth are pitiful, but they are rooted in the authority of bitter experience, and they are not shallow.

> —Sarah Beebe Fryer, "Beneath the Mask: The Plight of Daisy Buchanan," *Fitzgerald's New Women: Harbingers of Change* (Ann Arbor, MI: UMI Research Press, 1988), pp. 48–49

♣

JEROME MANDEL ON *THE GREAT GATSBY* AS A MEDIEVAL
ROMANCE

[Jerome Mandel (b. 1937) is a leading scholar on
medieval literature and author of *Alternative Readings
in Old English Poetry* (1987) and *Geoffrey Chaucer:
Building the Fragments of* The Canterbury Tales (1992).
In this extract, Mandel shows that *The Great Gatsby*
features many of the characteristics of the medieval
romance, with its aristocratic characters and its embodiment of the theme of courtly love.]

Medieval romance is an aristocratic genre. Perhaps that's why
it appealed to Fitzgerald. Medieval romance is about lords and
ladies, kings and princesses, warrior-knights who strive for
fame in the world, and the ladies who encourage them to ever
greater accomplishment. The steaming masses of the poor do
not appear except as servants. Fitzgerald writes about the
modern version of the medieval nobility: that aristocratic class
in American society privy to "the shining secrets that only
Midas and Morgan and Maecenas knew," who live, like Tom
Buchanan, in "white palaces" or, like Gatsby, in "a factual imitation of some Hôtel de Ville in Normandy, with a tower on one
side."

The most famous of these lords is Tom Buchanan, who was
"a national figure in a way" and whose "family were enormous-
ly wealthy." His inherited wealth and position, his old ivy, his
genuine Georgian mansion, his gift of pearls "valued at three
hundred and fifty thousand dollars," his command of horses—
all establish his noble credentials among those he calls "the
dominant race." With his "arrogant eyes," "supercilious man-
ner," and "appearance of always leaning aggressively forward,"
he is the most aristocratic figure in the novel. He treats people
with "paternal contempt." Tom is not only socially and eco-
nomically powerful but physically powerful as well. "A great
pack of muscle" gives his body "enormous power" and "lever-
age" that allows him to manipulate Nick Carraway, to turn him
about "imperatively", and to compel him from room to room.
Tom Buchanan is the king-figure in *The Great Gatsby*. His
domain is large. Not only does he maintain established resi-

dence in both East Egg and New York, but he also controls the whole world, drifting "unrestfully wherever people played polo and were rich together": Chicago, Louisville, three months in the South Seas, Santa Barbara, "a year in France"—at Cannes and Deauville—and then Kapiolani, the rest of Europe, East Egg, New York, and Europe again. He has Italian gardens and French windows. Gatsby wanders, fundamentally rootless; Nick Carraway migrates, first east then west. But no other character in the novel has so detailed an itinerary or so great a command of the world as Tom Buchanan.

The queen of this world is Daisy Fay, a position she holds both in her own right and as Tom's wife. She is not only identified as superior ("by far the most popular of all the young girls in Louisville"), but her royalty is also suggested by her splendid house, which has "the largest of the banners and the largest of the lawns." Nick Carraway refers to her as "the king's daughter, the golden girl" and recognizes "her membership in a rather distinguished secret society to which she and Tom belonged." Like Tom, she commands the whole world: she has "been everywhere and seen everything and done everything." Her experience and her privileged position in the world affirm both her aristocracy and her royalty. She and Tom are the "remotely rich"—royalty completely distanced and insulated from ordinary human concerns.

In this world of lords and ladies, Nick Carraway and Gatsby are knights, although only Nick is noble. From the beginning Fitzgerald establishes Nick Carraway's aristocracy in the American terms appropriate to the novel. His "family have been prominent, well-to-do people . . . for three generations"; they are, we are told, "something of a clan," reputedly (perhaps a bit facetiously) "descended from the Dukes of Buccleuch." And, moreover, Nick is cousin to the Queen. In medieval romance, blood will always tell. No matter how down-and-out a nobleman may be, he will always, and quickly, rise to his rightful position in society—as Tristan does when he is abandoned on the coast of Cornwall. Nick Carraway is in the East only a few days before he, too, is looked upon as "an original settler." Often a mere change of clothes reveals the nobleman's true identity (compare Rual li Foitenant in *Tristan*). But no change of clothes can make a nobleman out of Gatsby. He is the *parvenu,* the medieval country-boy trying to pass himself off as someone he is not. He has no noble antecedents. He "sprang from his Platonic conception of himself." Gatsby only looks like a gentleman—to Wolfsheim. Tom sees through the invention and the gorgeous clothes immediately, and he ruthlessly though accurately identifies Gatsby as "some big bootlegger." Gatsby can be neither a gentleman nor an Oxford man because "he wears a pink suit."

Although not an aristocrat, Gatsby is a great warrior, perhaps in the mold of Sir John Hawkwood and The White Company. He "did extraordinarily well" "in that delayed Teutonic migration known as the Great War." He began as a first lieutenant, "was a captain before he went to the front," was promoted to major, and was honored by "little Montenegro." In medieval terms, Gatsby returned one of the victors from the Great European Tournament of 1918, whereas Nick Carraway merely participated.

Medieval knights are lovers as well as warriors. World War One allowed Gatsby to establish both his heroic credentials and his validity as a courtly lover. As such Gatsby's only interest in money, fame, and success is to get his beloved to notice him. To impress his beloved, a medieval knight risked his life to win tournaments and to gain fame in the world: Cligés, to cite one of many obvious examples, "feels his luck has come, when he can display his chivalry and bravery openly before her who is his very life." That is why Gatsby entertains so lavishly: he wants to attract and to impress. He hopes Daisy will "wander into one of his parties, some night." "He wants her to see his house" and his shirts. He revalues everything according to her response. When Daisy is "offended" and "appalled" by the parties, "the whole caravansary" collapses "like a card house at the disapproval in her eyes." In this, as in everything, the beloved's attitude determines the courtly lover's behavior.

—Jerome Mandel, "The Grotesque Rose: Medieval Romance and *The Great Gatsby," Modern Fiction Studies* 34, No. 4 (Winter 1988): 544–47

JOYCE A. ROWE ON GATSBY'S RELATIONSHIP WITH NICK
CARRAWAY

[Joyce A. Rowe is a professor of English at Fordham
University and the author of *Equivocal Endings in
Classic American Novels* (1988), from which the following extract is taken. Here, Rowe studies the relationship of Gatsby with Nick Carraway, finding that
despite their many differences the two characters share
a number of attitudes in common.]

That Gatsby is not just the mythic embodiment of an American
type but personifies the outline of our national consciousness is
demonstrated by his structural relation to the other characters
and, in particular, to the narrator, Nick Carraway.

Despite differences of class and taste, despite their apparent
mutually antagonistic purposes, all the characters in this book
are defined by their nostalgia for and sense of betrayal by some
lost, if only dimly apprehended promise in their past—a sense
of life's possibilities toward which only Gatsby has retained the
ingenuous faith and energy of the true seeker. It is in the differ-
ence between vision and sight, between the longing for self-
transcendence and the lust for immediate gain—for sexual,
financial, or social domination—that Nick, his chronicler and
witness, finds the moral distinction which separates Gatsby
from the "foul dust" of the others who float in his wake. And
this moral dichotomy runs through the structure of the entire
work. For the rapacious nature of each of the others, whether
crude, desperate, arrogant or false, is finally shown to be a
function of their common loss of vision, their blurred or dis-
placed sense of possibilities—punningly symbolized in the
enormous empty retinas of the occulist-wag, Dr T. J. Eckleburg.
Thus Gatsby and those who eddy around him are, reciprocally,
positive and negative images of one another; but whether
faithless or true all are doomed by the wasteful, self-deluding
nature of the longing which controls their lives and which
when it fails leaves its adherents utterly naked and alone, "con-
tiguous to nothing."

However, Nick's insight into the distinction between Gatsby
and others does not free him from his own involvement in the

world he observes. His acute awareness of his own self-division (toward Gatsby as toward all the others) turns out to be the mirror inversion of his subject's unconscious one; it accounts for the sympathetic bond between them. And just as Gatsby's ingenuous self-dissociation is the ground of his faith that the moral complexity of the world can be subdued to his imaginative vision (Daisy's feelings for Tom are only a case of the "personal"), so Nick's self-division leads him to ultimately reject the world ("I wanted no more . . . privileged glimpses into the human heart"). They are twin poles of All or Nothing—Gatsby's hope is Nick's despair.

Nick's kinship to Gatsby is established in the prologue, where his own version of "infinite hope"—the capacity to reserve judgment—is implicitly contrasted with Gatsby's "extraordinary gift for hope." This latter is not, says Nick, in a self-deprecating reference, a matter of any "flabby impressionability," but of a romantic readiness such as he has never found in any other person "and which it is not likely I shall ever find again." The phrase tells us that Nick too is a seeker, that the strength of Gatsby's romantic energy resonates against Nick's own muted but responsive sensibility. Indeed, Nick's most immediately distinguishing trait, his consciousness of the flux of time as a series of intense, irrecoverable moments, is keyed to a romantic pessimism whose melancholy note is struck on his thirtieth birthday, when he envisions his future as a burden of diminishing returns leading inexorably to loneliness, enervation, and death.

Moreover, it is Nick's own confused responsiveness to his cousin's sexual power and charm that allows him subsequently to understand Gatsby's equation of Daisy with all that is most desirable under the heavens—ultimately with the siren song of the American continent. Nick cannot help but be compelled by the buoyant vitality which surrounds her and the glowing sound of her "low, thrilling voice," which sings with "a promise that she had done gay, exciting things just a while since and that there were gay exciting things hovering in the next hour." But, as the shadow of his double, Nick's response to Daisy is qualified by his discomforting awareness of the illusory and deceptive in her beauty. Her smirking insincerity, her banal chatter, the alluring whiteness of her expensive clothes—most of all, the languid boredom which enfolds her life—suggest a willing captivity, a lazy self-submission to a greater power than her own magical charms: the extraordinary wealth and physical arrogance that enable Tom Buchanan to dominate her. And Nick's visceral dislike for the man Daisy has given herself to, fanned by his intellectual and moral scorn for Tom's crude attempt to master "ideas" as he does horses and women, allies him with, as it prefigures, Gatsby's bland disregard of Tom as a factor in Daisy's existence.

—Joyce A. Rowe, *Equivocal Endings in Classic American Novels* (Cambridge: Cambridge University Press, 1988), pp. 107–9

RICHARD LEHAN ON FITZGERALD, T. S. ELIOT, AND OSWALD SPENGLER

[Richard Lehan (b. 1930) is a professor of English at the University of California at Los Angeles and author of *F. Scott Fitzgerald and the Craft of Fiction* (1966) and *Theodore Dreiser: His World and His Novels* (1969). In the following extract, taken from his book on *The Great Gatsby,* Lehan explores the relationship of the novel to T. S. Eliot's *The Waste Land* (1922) and to Oswald Spengler's historical treatise, *The Decline of the West* (German edition 1918–22; English translation 1926–28), all of which discuss the notion that this phase of Western civilization was coming to an end.]

The Waste Land was Eliot's response to a postwar Europe experiencing radical change. Historically, one empire after another had fallen, the last being the Hapsburgs, with Great Britain in line to be the next "falling tower." Eliot depicts a world coming morally apart, a world that has no principle to hold it together. We see the rich with nerves on end; middle-class housewives caught entrapped in sterile and purposeless lives; and lower-class clerks seeking mere gratification, no matter how mechanical or unfulfilling.

All of these people are culturally empty. Like Henry Adams, Eliot believed that every society needed some kind of mythic meaning to give it center and direction; an obsession for profit was not enough. Man had lost his primitive energy, had lost the basis for the Fisher King whose sacrificial vitality had been handed down in the form of Osiris, Adonis, Atiz, Tamuz, to Christ. Their vitality was now being played out, exhausted, in the post-Enlightenment world of science and technology. Gatsby brings the intensity of this lost vision to life, complete with its religious nature, something we know from Fitzgerald's original conception of the novel and from our own analysis of its religious motifs. Such intensity takes on a romantic vitality that Gatsby incarnates in Dan Cody and Daisy Fay. At the moment when the *idea* of Dan Cody can no longer hold Gatsby's world together, Gatsby tells Nick "the strange story of his youth and Dan Cody—told it to me because 'Jay Gatsby' had broken up like glass against Tom's hard malice, and the long secret extravaganza was played out." At the moment Gatsby is deprived of such intensity, his imaginative conception of self becomes exhausted and the world around him changes before his eyes: the resplendent gives way to "an unfamiliar sky" whose materiality brings a shiver.

This sense of the exhaustion of romantic possibility was inseparable from the postwar sense of world weariness that we find in both the story that Nick Carraway tells and in the story Tiresias tells in *The Waste Land*. Eliot in turn drew upon Hermann Hesse's *Blick ins Chaos*. But the work that perhaps most subsumes both Fitzgerald's and Eliot's statements is one that we have already discussed, Spengler's *Decline of the West*. The sense of both religious and romantic intensity that Eliot and Fitzgerald felt slipping away, Spengler saw embodied in Faustian man, whose spirit was also being exhausted: "Force, Will, has an aim," Spengler tells us, "and where there is an aim there is for the inquiring eye an end. . . . The Faust . . . is dying. . . . What the myth of Götterdämmerung signified of old, the irreligious form of it, the theory of Entropy, signifies today." The change of terminology here is important: to move from the idea of romantic depletion (as suggested in metaphors of waste and ashes) to the idea of entropy moves the discussion from a religious/mythic context to the scientific one involving

entropy. Entropy results when, in a closed system, molecules become uniform and lose their capacity to do work. The application of Newton's second law of thermodynamics remotely interested even Tom Buchanan in his discussions of whether the sun is heating up or cooling down.
— Richard Lehan, *The Great Gatsby: The Limits of Wonder* (Boston: Twayne, 1990), pp. 94–96

ANDREW HOOK ON TOM BUCHANAN

[Andrew Hook (b. 1932) is Bradley Professor of English Literature at the University of Glasgow, Scotland. He has written *Scotland and America: A Study of Cultural Relations* (1975) and edited *Dos Passos: A Collection of Critical Essays* (1974). In this extract, from his book on Fitzgerald, Hook studies the character of Tom Buchanan; he disputes the standard contention that Tom is meant to be contrasted with Gatsby on a social level, finding that both characters are representative of the *nouveau riche* ("recently wealthy") in American society.]

Tom Buchanan is one of Fitzgerald's most brilliant creations. Tom's brutal unattractiveness—all his life has been an anticlimax since he played end for the Yale University football team— seems to keep a considerable degree of reader sympathy with Daisy. Tom's attitudes, his racism and bigotry, his insensitivity, and his behaviour, do make Daisy's cynicism understandable. Ultimately, however, Tom and Daisy are on the same side, representing a harsh reality always liable to shatter the visionary world of 'Jay Gatsby.' Near the beginning of the novel, Nick feels that he is manipulated emotionally by Daisy in such a way that he is made to recognize 'her membership in a rather distinguished secret society to which she and Tom belonged.' At the end of the novel, despite everything that Gatsby can do, Daisy and Tom are back together, members as it were of that same secret society. After the climactic scene in the Plaza Hotel in New York, and after the accident in which Myrtle Wilson is killed, Nick sees Tom and Daisy sitting together around their kitchen table: 'There was an unmistakable air of natural intimacy about the picture, and anybody would have said that they were conspiring together.' Earlier, in the Plaza Hotel scene, Gatsby had made his final effort to repeat the past—to win Daisy back, to blot out the five years of marriage to Tom, to recreate Daisy in his own image as the unwavering lover. But it cannot be done. Time and ordinary human realities come together to expose the fatuity and hopelessness of Gatsby's yearnings. Bewildered, Gatsby thinks it is Tom's accusations that are preventing Daisy joining him. He begins to defend himself:

> . . . he began to talk excitedly to Daisy, denying everything, defending his name against accusations that had not been made. But with every word she was drawing further and further into herself, so he gave that up, and only the dead dream fought on as the afternoon slipped away, trying to touch what was no longer tangible, struggling unhappily, undespairingly, toward that lost voice across the room.

What it is important to recognize is that Gatsby's inevitable defeat here involves the nature of reality itself. There is of course a sense in which *The Great Gatsby* is a novel of manners: it does comment on American society in the 1920s and it is critical of the corruption and moral disorder of the period. Jordan Baker's cheating at golf, just as much as the valley of ashes, in which the Wilsons' garage is situated, is an image of that corruption and disorder. And in this area there is little to choose between Gatsby and the Buchanans: if Gatsby is involved in the criminality of bootleg liquor and financial swindling, the Buchanans belong to a world which is selfish, careless, amoral and irresponsible. That it is Daisy who is driving the car that kills Myrtle Wilson is entirely appropriate: 'They were careless people, Tom and Daisy—they smashed up things and creatures and then retreated back into their money or their vast carelessness, or whatever it was that kept them together, and let other people clean up the mess they had made. . . .' Readings of the novel that try to discriminate between Gatsby and the Buchanans in terms of new and old money are thus misconceived. The Buchanans in no way represent some kind of old world aristocracy into which the nouveau riche Gatsby is trying to gatecrash. Tom Buchanan's present of a three hundred and fifty thousand dollar pearl necklace to Daisy on their wedding is of entirely the same order as Gatsby's palatial mansion. Tom and Daisy are quite capable of being snobbish about Gatsby and his behaviour—but that does not mean that they are members of an American aristocracy. If there is such a thing it exists, like Anson Hunter's family in 'The Rich Boy,' only in the East—certainly not in the Middle West from which all the central characters in *The Great Gatsby* derive.

—Andrew Hook, *F. Scott Fitzgerald* (London: Edward Arnold, 1992), pp. 56–58

Books by
F. Scott Fitzgerald

This Side of Paradise. 1920.

Flappers and Philosophers. 1920.

The St. Paul Daily Dirge. 1922.

The Beautiful and Damned. 1922.

Tales of the Jazz Age. 1922.

The Vegetable; or, From President to Postman. 1923.

The Great Gatsby. 1925.

All the Sad Young Men. 1926.

John Jackson's Arcady. Ed. Lilian Holmes Strack. 1928.

Tender Is the Night: A Romance. 1934.

The True Story of Appomattox. 1934.

Taps at Reveille. 1935.

The Last Tycoon: An Unfinished Novel; Together with The Great Gatsby and Selected Stories. Ed. Edmund Wilson. 1941.

The Crack-Up (with others). Ed. Edmund Wilson. 1945.

The Portable F. Scott Fitzgerald. Ed. Dorothy Parker. 1945.

Stories. Ed. Malcolm Cowley. 1951.

Turkey Remains and How to Inter Them. 1956.

Afternoon of an Author: A Selection of Uncollected Stories and Essays. Ed. Arthur Mizener. 1957.

The Bodley Head F. Scott Fitzgerald. 1958–63. 6 vols.

The Mystery of the Raymond Mortgage. 1960.

The Pat Hobby Stories. Ed. Arnold Gingrich. 1962.

Stories. 1962–68. 5 vols.

The Fitzgerald Reader. Ed. Arthur Mizener. 1963.

Letters. Ed. Andrew Turnbull. 1963.

The Apprentice Fiction of F. Scott Fitzgerald 1909–1917. Ed. John Kuehl. 1965.

Thoughtbook of Francis Scott Key Fitzgerald. 1965.

Letters to His Daughter. Ed. Andrew Turnbull. 1965.

Dearly Beloved: A Short Story. 1969.

F. Scott Fitzgerald in His Own Time: A Miscellany. Ed. Matthew J. Bruccoli and Jackson R. Bryer. 1971.

Dear Scott/Dear Max: The Fitzgerald-Perkins Correspondence (with Maxwell Perkins). Ed. John Kuehl and Jackson R. Bryer. 1971.

As Ever, Scott Fitz—: Letters between F. Scott Fitzgerald and His Literary Agent Harold Ober 1919–1940. Ed. Matthew J. Bruccoli and Jennifer McCabe Atkinson. 1972.

F. Scott Fitzgerald's Ledger: A Facsimile. 1972.

The Basil and Josephine Stories. Ed. Jackson R. Bryer and John Kuehl. 1973.

The Great Gatsby: A Facsimile of the Manuscript. Ed. Matthew J. Bruccoli. 1973.

Bits of Paradise: 21 Uncollected Stories by F. Scott and Zelda Fitzgerald. Ed. Scottie Fitzgerald Smith and Matthew J. Bruccoli. 1973.

Preface to This Side of Paradise. Ed. John R. Hopkins. 1975.

The Cruise of the Rolling Junk. 1976.

Screenplay for Three Comrades *by Erich Maria Remarque.* Ed. Matthew J. Bruccoli. 1978.

Notebooks. Ed. Matthew J. Bruccoli. 1978.

St. Paul Plays 1911–1914. Ed. Alan Margolies. 1978.

The Price Was High: The Last Uncollected Stories. Ed. Matthew J. Bruccoli. 1979.

Correspondence. Ed. Matthew J. Bruccoli and Margaret M. Duggan. 1980.

Poems 1911–1940. Ed. Matthew J. Bruccoli. 1981.

F. Scott Fitzgerald on Writing. Ed. Larry W. Phillips. 1985.

Works (Cambridge Edition). Ed. Matthew J. Bruccoli. 1991– .

The Love of the Last Tycoon: A Western. Ed. Matthew J. Bruccoli. 1993.

Babylon Revisited: The Screenplay. 1993.

A Life in Letters. Ed. Matthew J. Bruccoli. 1994.

Works about Fitzgerald and The Great Gatsby

Aldridge, John W. "The Life of Gatsby." In Aldridge's *Time to Murder and Create: The Contemporary Novel in Crisis.* New York: David McKay, 1966, pp. 192–218.

Berman, Ronald. The Great Gatsby *and Modern Times.* Urbana: University of Illinois Press, 1994.

Bewley, Marius. "Scott Fitzgerald's Criticism of America." *Sewanee Review* 62 (1954): 223–46.

Bloom, Harold, ed. *Gatsby.* New York: Chelsea House, 1990.

———, ed. *F. Scott Fitzgerald's* The Great Gatsby. New York: Chelsea House, 1986.

Breitwieser, Mitchell. "*The Great Gatsby:* Grief, Jazz and the Eye-Witness." *Arizona Quarterly* 47 (1991): 17–70.

Bruccoli, Matthew J. *Fitzgerald and Hemingway: A Dangerous Friendship.* New York: Carroll & Graf, 1994.

———. *Some Sort of Epic Grandeur: The Life of F. Scott Fitzgerald.* New York: Harcourt Brace Jovanovich, 1981.

Bufkin, E. C. "A Pattern of Parallel and Double: The Function of Myrtle in *The Great Gatsby.*" *Modern Fiction Studies* 14 (1968–69): 517–24.

Callahan, John F. *The Illusions of a Nation: Myth and History in the Novels of F. Scott Fitzgerald.* Urbana: University of Illinois Press, 1972.

Chambers, John B. *The Novels of F. Scott Fitzgerald.* New York: St. Martin's Press, 1989.

Claridge, Henry, ed. *F. Scott Fitzgerald: Critical Assessments.* Mountfield, UK: Helm Information, 1991. 4 vols.

Corso, Joseph. "One Not-Forgotten Summer Night: Sources for Fictional Symbols of American Character in *The Great Gatsby.*" *Fitzgerald/Hemingway Annual 1976,* pp. 8–33.

Cross, K. W. F. *F. Scott Fitzgerald.* Edinburgh: Oliver & Boyd, 1964.

Dillon, Andrew. *"The Great Gatsby:* The Vitality of Illusion." *Arizona Quarterly* 44 (1988): 49–61.

Donaldson, Scott. *Fool for Love: F. Scott Fitzgerald.* New York: Congdon & Weed, 1983.

————, ed. *Critical Essays on F. Scott Fitzgerald's* The Great Gatsby. Boston: G. K. Hall, 1984.

Eble, Kenneth. *F. Scott Fitzgerald.* New York: Twayne, 1963.

Elmore, A. E. *"The Great Gatsby* as Well Wrought Urn." In *Modern American Fiction: Form and Function,* ed. Thomas Daniel Young. Baton Rouge: Louisiana State University Press, 1989, pp. 57–92.

Fahey, William A. *F. Scott Fitzgerald and the American Dream.* New York: Thomas Y. Crowell Co., 1973.

Gallo, Rose Adrienne. *F. Scott Fitzgerald.* New York: Frederick Ungar Publishing Co., 1978.

Hindus, Milton. *F. Scott Fitzgerald: An Introduction and Interpretation.* New York: Holt, Rinehart & Winston, 1968.

Hoffman, Frederick J., ed. The Great Gatsby: *A Study.* New York: Scribner's, 1962.

Holquist, Michael. "Stereotyping in Autobiography and Historiography: Colonialism in *The Great Gatsby." Poetics Today* 9 (1988): 453–72.

Lee, A. Robert. "'A Quality of Distortion': Imagining in *The Great Gatsby."* In *Scott Fitzgerald: The Promises of Life,* ed. A. Robert Lee. London: Vision Press; New York: St. Martin's Press, 1989, pp. 37–60.

Lehan, Richard D. *F. Scott Fitzgerald and the Craft of Fiction.* Carbondale: Southern Illinois University Press, 1966.

Le Vot, André. *F. Scott Fitzgerald: A Biography.* Translated by William Byron. Garden City, NY: Doubleday, 1983.

Long, Robert Emmet. *The Achieving of* The Great Gatsby: *F. Scott Fitzgerald 1920–1925.* Lewisburg, PA: Bucknell University Press, 1979.

Lynn, David H. *The Hero's Tale: Narrators in the Early Modern Novel.* Basingstoke, UK: Macmillan Press, 1989.

Magistrale, Tony, and Mary Jane Dickerson. "The Language of Time in *The Great Gatsby.*" *College Literature* 16 (1989): 117–28.

Mangum, Bryant. *A Fortune Yet: Money in the Art of F. Scott Fitzgerald.* New York: Garland, 1991.

Meyers, Jeffrey. *Scott Fitzgerald: A Biography.* New York: HarperCollins, 1994.

Mizener, Arthur. *The Far Side of Paradise: A Biography of F. Scott Fitzgerald.* Boston: Houghton Mifflin, 1951.

O'Meara, Lauraleigh. "Medium of Exchange: The Blue Coupé Dialogue in *The Great Gatsby.*" *Papers on Language and Literature* 30 (1994): 73–87.

Parker, David. "*The Great Gatsby:* Two Versions of the Hero." *English Studies* 54 (1973): 37–51.

Parr, Susan Resneck. "Individual Responsibility in *The Great Gatsby.*" *Virginia Quarterly Review* 57 (1981): 662–80.

Pauly, Thomas H. "Gatsby as Gangster." *Studies in American Fiction* 21 (1993): 225–36.

Pendleton, Thomas A. *I'm Sorry about the Clock: Chronology, Composition, and Narrative Technique in* The Great Gatsby. Selinsgrove, PA: Susquehanna University Press, 1993.

Phillips, Gene D. *Fiction, Film, and F. Scott Fitzgerald.* Chicago: Loyola University Press, 1986.

Piper, Henry Dan. *F. Scott Fitzgerald: A Critical Portrait.* New York: Holt, Rinehart & Winston, 1965.

Rohrkemper, John. "The Allusive Past: Historical Perspective in *The Great Gatsby.*" *College Literature* 12 (1985): 153–62.

Sheffield, R. Michael. "The Temporal Location of Fitzgerald's Jay Gatsby." *Texas Quarterly* 18, No. 2 (Summer 1975): 122–30.

Sipiora, Phillip. "Vampires of the Heart: Gender Trouble in *The Great Gatsby.*" In *The Aching Hearth: Family Violence in Life and Literature,* ed. Sara Munson Deats and Lagretta Tallent Lenker. New York: Insight Books, 1991, pp. 199–220.

Sklar, Robert. *F. Scott Fitzgerald: The Last Laocoön*. New York: Oxford University Press, 1967.

Stavola, Thomas J. *Scott Fitzgerald: Crisis in an American Identity*. London: Vision Press, 1979.

Stern, Milton R. *The Golden Moment: The Novels of F. Scott Fitzgerald*. Urbana: University of Illinois Press, 1970.

Trilling, Lionel. "F. Scott Fitzgerald." In Trilling's *The Liberal Imagination*. New York: Viking Press, 1950, pp. 243–54.

Way, Brian. *F. Scott Fitzgerald and the Art of Social Fiction*. New York: St. Martin's Press, 1980.

White, Patti. *Gatsby's Party: The System and the List in Contemporary Narrative*. West Lafayette, IN: Purdue University Press, 1992.

Whitley, John S. *F. Scott Fitzgerald: The Great Gatsby*. London: Edward Arnold, 1976.

Wilson, Robert N. "F. Scott Fitzgerald: Personality and Culture." In Wilson's *The Writer as Social Seer*. Chapel Hill: University of North Carolina Press, 1979, pp. 17–41.

Index of
Themes and Ideas